EUROPE
2030

EUROPE★
2030 DANIEL BENJAMIN
editor

BROOKINGS INSTITUTION PRESS
Washington, D.C.

Daniel Benjamin completed work on this book while at Brookings Institution and before moving to a position with the U.S. Department of State. The book does not represent the views of the State Department or the U.S. government.

Library of Congress Cataloging in Publication data
Europe 2030 / Daniel Benjamin, editor.
     p.   cm.
  Includes index.
  Summary: "Contributors, with insight and drawing on in-depth knowledge of European affairs over the last forty years, describe the European Union's current strengths and weaknesses and forecast its future development"--Provided by publisher.
  ISBN 978-0-8157-0280-1 (pbk. : alk. paper)
  1. European Union--Forecasting. 2. European Union countries--Politics and government--21st century. I. Benjamin, Daniel, 1961- II. Title: Europe twenty-thirty. III. Series.
  JN30.E82482 2010
  341.242'20112--dc22   2009052537

9 8 7 6 5 4 3 2 1

Printed on acid-free paper

Typeset in Sabon with Frutiger display

Composition by Peter Lindeman
Arlington, Virginia

Printed by R. R. Donnelley
Harrisonburg, Virginia

Contents

Foreword

HOW WILL THE European Union look twenty years from now?

It is practically impossible to give an answer. The purpose of this book is more reasonable: to find out from its authors which are the main issues at stake in 2030 Europe. The future cannot be described, however, since the dominant factors necessarily will include normative perceptions. That is why we have asked for essays and not forecasts.

For the smaller European countries, even more so than the larger member states, the shape that Europe will take over the next couple of decades and how it will arrive there are decisive. That explains how fundamental these kinds of exercises are for Portugal's future, and explains, too, the interest of the Luso-American Foundation in organizing and sponsoring this initiative. I am very grateful to my friends Philip Gordon, Daniel Benjamin, and José Cutileiro, and the support given by the Brookings Institution. With their commitment, it was possible to gather some of the most talented minds with expertise in European affairs and have them try and imagine how Europe will be in the near future. The outcome was not disappointing. On the contrary, the analyses made and the insights offered were deep and provided considerable food for thought.

My reading of the contributions reinforced my conviction that the European Union will remain a polity without a constitutional *demos;* a confederation of states that share part of their sovereignty powers. However, its responsiveness to external factors, economic and political, will increase the confederation's powers. Competition with the United States and the threats and challenges posed by many parts of the rest of the world will force Europe to respond, changing its structure and becoming more federalist, in order to survive and play a critical role in international affairs. This is what can be called the reactive model of progress in European integration.

The uncertainties are many, and we cannot neglect the positive and negative influences of the internal factors. I dare say that had Gorbachev arrived later, we might have seen even greater progress toward European collaboration with its eastern partners. Other readers may conclude otherwise, but that is the type of discussion that the chapters here are aiming at and one that will help to serve European policymakers in the years ahead.

Rui Chancerelle de Machete
Lisbon, Portugal
January 2010

Preface

FIRST, I wish to congratulate the Fundação Luso-Americana para o Desenvolvimento and the Brookings Institution for their support of such an important initiative. And it is a great pleasure, with this preface, to be included among such a distinguished company of authors.

Now, the question remains, how are we preparing the European Union to face the challenges of the twenty-first century? The future starts today. The decisions we make now will determine the shape of the EU to come.

A key point to keep in mind is the immense potential of the enlarged European Union—twenty-seven member states and half a billion people—stretching from the Atlantic Ocean and the Mediterranean Sea to the Baltic Sea. Enlargement has been a great success not only in terms of European integration, but also in the context of European history. The peaceful unification of the continent will certainly be seen as one of the greatest achievements of our generation. Acting together, we can make the European Union an impressive force in global politics.

In fifty years the EU has come a long way and is now playing a decisive role in world affairs. Let me give a few examples. Today, it is leading both the global effort to combat the financial and the economic crises, in the G-20 context, as well as the international fight against climate change. The economic crisis has shown that we need renewed international rules. Global transformations at the financial, economic, environmental, and social levels were not accompanied by the creation of adequate rules and institutions. World leaders must fill the gap. I believe that we need more, not less, globalization. We must resist the temptation of protectionism. Rather, the world needs a normative globalization—a process of establishing common principles and rules that will make the most of the beneficial transnational economic forces that have helped bring millions out of poverty. Together with its partners, the EU will work to promote regional stability and a new global economic order, to pursue open trade, to fight climate change, and to promote development and good governance.

In the coming decades, the EU will be a major shaper of the institutions and rules of global governance. Given its experience in transnational governance, the EU is well-positioned to promote the principles of openness and multilateralism on a global level. I am sure that the EU, but also the European Commission in particular, will continue to play a major role in the renewal of multilateral institutions.

The prosperity of Europe, as a major world trader, exporter, and investor, rests heavily on its economic and trade relations with the rest of the world. That is why we believe open and fair trade is the way to address the current crisis and to make Europe more prosperous. Europe will also continue to lead in promoting economic and social development for the world's poorest. In particular, I hope that relations between Europe and Africa will be further intensified.

The twenty-first-century world will probably see power distributed more widely than during previous centuries. However, we must guard against multipolarity leading to geopolitical and geoeconomic conflicts and disputes, which could endanger world peace. We need to strengthen multilateralism and international cooperation. The multipolar conflicts and wars of the first half of the twentieth century should serve as a lesson to the world. At the very least, Europe has a central role in ensuring the 2030s will be considerably more peaceful than the 1930s.

To help create a better world, but also to defend European interests and European values, the EU has continued to forge partnerships with other global powers. I am confident that it will build on those partnerships and develop deeper and more ambitious relations with emerging powers such as China, India, and Brazil. With Russia, too, its largest neighbor, the EU must build a comprehensive and cooperative relationship, particularly with regard to energy and our common neighborhood.

A special word on transatlantic relations: the arrival of the new American administration will strengthen a common Atlantic agenda for globalization. In the twenty-first century, a strong transatlantic partnership may not be sufficient, but it is certainly a necessary condition to tackle global challenges. The transatlantic Economic Council, set up in 2007, could serve as the foundation as the United States and Europe work together to create a real common transatlantic economic space.

In the area of defense, Europe and the United States share common challenges, and recent developments regarding relations between NATO and the EU are welcome. They offer an opportunity to reinforce a common European defense identity that is not in contradiction, but complements the transatlantic alliance. In fact, our American friends are asking us to strengthen our defense and security dimensions, and I believe Europe should do more in this area.

Europe's ability to shape world politics and globalization also has a strong internal dimension. In this century, it is not possible to separate external affairs from internal issues. If the ability to act effectively in the world starts from within Europe, in terms of institutions and political will, it is also true that our internal prosperity and security start abroad.

The type of Europe where European citizens will live will be determined by the kind of world Europeans shape. Peace, democracy, freedom, economic prosperity, and social justice require an open EU fully engaged in the world. With the Treaty of Lisbon, which came into force on December 1, 2009, the European Union will be far better equipped to play this role and act in a more efficient way on the world stage. Yet, the institutional capacity to act is not enough. Europe also needs the political will. Leadership at all levels will be essential.

José Manuel Durão Barroso
President, European Commission
January 2010

JOSCHKA FISCHER 1

Europe 2030: Global Power or Hamster on a Wheel?

TWENTY YEARS CAN be a very long time in politics, but it is a very short period in terms of historical change. The European Union (EU), a political entity entirely without historical precedent, embodies that paradox of stasis and change. Indeed, one might call the EU an institutionalized contradiction: it functions, even though, in theory, it should not.

For states on the European continent, the EU embodies a new political system, the second since the international system that prevailed since the seventeenth-century's Peace of Westphalia destroyed itself in the twentieth century's two world wars. Then, during the five decades of the cold war, Europe was defined politically by the bipolar world order to which the conflict between East and West gave rise. Europe was the stage upon which the global confrontation between the United States and the Soviet Union, between freedom and dictatorship, and between capitalism and communism played out.

When, in 1989, the Iron Curtain unexpectedly fell and the Soviet Union disintegrated, Europe's bipolar system was finished as well. In its place was established the EU's model of integration, which relied on NATO's survival and thus on a continuing U.S. security guarantee for Europe. Even today, Europeans, accustomed to infighting, are in no position to ensure their own protection and are unwilling to bear the burdens necessary to do so. The United States may not be a formal member state, but it is de facto a part of the EU, indispensable to Europe's system of integration and its ability to sustain itself in the post–cold war era.

And yet that system does not follow any known model of national or international law. The EU is neither a union of sovereign states nor a federation or a confederation—and much less a federal state. It is a completely new entity, sui generis. The nearest definition of the EU's character is that of a "composite of states," in which the continued national sovereignty of the member states is combined with their obligations to European institutions, European law, and European policies—for example, to the common market, the agricultural market, the economic union, and the monetary union. To complicate matters further, eleven of the EU's twenty-seven member states do not belong to the monetary union, and Norway, a nonmember state, plays a role in policing the EU's external borders.

That complexity is not lost on the EU's 500 million citizens, and it poses a serious problem in a democracy: the tremendously intricate composite of European and national sovereignties and jurisdictions inspires more head scratching than it does emotional zeal, confidence, or identification. And that is at the heart of the EU's current crisis.

Contradictions are for intellectuals, not for politicians and political parties. Winning elections requires clear, consistent messages with which people can identify. Who would be willing to risk giving up his national family, his language, and the security of his country for one giant, incomprehensible question mark? Who would sacrifice himself for a cause that almost no one understands? France and the Netherlands answered those questions in 2005, in referendums that derailed the EU's draft constitution. And Ireland's referendum last year on that document's quasi-constitutional successor, the Lisbon Treaty, showed once again that when such questions are put to a popular vote, there simply is no majority for Europe.

ENVIED ABROAD, UNLOVED AT HOME

After 1989, there was a stampede toward the EU, which would recur if the union's doors were opened to neighboring nonmember states. I suspect that even Russia would jump at the chance to join. Certainly, other countries would: the Balkan states and Turkey, Ukraine, Georgia, perhaps Moldova, and Mediterranean states like Morocco and Israel.

And yet, while almost all of the EU's neighbors wish to join, its own citizens increasingly oppose not only further expansion but also deeper political integration. The EU guarantees economic development and prosperity, social and democratic stability, and, together with NATO, security for all its members. But as soon as those benefits are secured, most of its citizens seem to rediscover their inner parochial, favoring the exclusion of others and resisting European "encroachment" on national sovereignty.

Nevertheless, if any of the EU's member states were to hold a referendum on withdrawal from the union, a majority in favor would be found almost nowhere, except perhaps among the British (more precisely, the English). Even one of the continent's most trenchant and high-profile euroskeptics, Czech president Václav Klaus, does not speak for the overwhelming majority of his country's citizens on this issue.

Europe's national governments have a strong institutional incentive to orchestrate that political schizophrenia because the demand for democratic accountability continues to be concentrated at the national level. As a result, governments enact policies in the European Council that they then denounce to their own countries' press and parliaments as the "bureaucratic mistakes" and "overreaching" of Brussels. So their citizens, too, learn to reject the EU while embracing it.

Initially, the European unification process was not at all contradictory. It was conceived as a project for Europe's elite—governments, parliaments, and the bureaucracy. In other words, national interests would balance each other through new, transnational bureaucracies, institutions, and rules. The question of democratic validation played only a subordinate role, if any. *Historical* validation arose almost of its own accord: the Second World War was still a living memory for Western Europeans, and the Soviet threat defined a dangerous present. The widespread desire for a new order, and through it an end to Europe's fratricidal wars, meant that for the six founding members—Germany, France, Italy, and the Benelux countries—the attempt to achieve European unification needed no further justification.

By contrast, the rationale for the EU today is neither consistent nor self-evident. The EU's further development is blocked, as its bureaucratic-administrative and political effectiveness have now run up against the full weight of national tradition. Europe stagnates, even as it marches on. Consider, for example, the high level of efficiency and competence that produced the economic, social, and political success of the *Ost-erweiterung* (Eastern expansion), which took in ten new members in 2004, followed by Bulgaria and Romania in 2007. The introduction of the common currency and the subsequent expansion of the euro zone similarly attest to superior governance.

Yet, at the same time, the EU's lack of democratic validation is now, decades on, being acutely felt, particularly in its inability to craft a common external policy—witness, for example, the EU member states' failure to take a common stand on an EU strategy during the financial crisis or the recognition of Kosovo. And as European nations proceed down the path of integration into this curious composite entity, the lack of sufficient mechanisms of democratic validation will inevitably erode the EU's internal effectiveness and stability as well. Indeed, it is a deficiency that threatens to sidetrack every further development that requires an amendment of the EU treaty—that is, national ratification. As the uncertain fate of the Lisbon Treaty suggests, the dog of Europe, which has been biting its own tail over institutional reform for almost two decades, may be prepared to do so for another generation.

NO SUPER-STATE

The European nations, with their various languages, cultures, and narratives, are all about 1,000 years old. Their differentiation constitutes Europe's essence, its character, and its reality—and thus the essence, character, and reality of the EU. To believe that these historically determined realities will melt and then be homogenized by the churning force of integration is to indulge in sheer fantasy.

As a result, the tension between the EU and its member states cannot be overcome through a federation. Instead, the EU must assume those parts of traditional national sovereignty that the common market has rendered functionally obsolete for small European nation states, as well as those needed to ensure a lasting peace on the European continent while excluding any hegemony.

The EU has thus far fulfilled its obligations: it has achieved economic success through the common market, European law, monetary union, and the removal of rigid internal borders within the Schengen area. The EU also functions almost perfectly as a framework for peace: because its structure weakens the larger, more powerful members and strengthens the smaller, less powerful states, all are compelled to balance and bargain over their interests constantly. That prevents the rise of any internal hegemonic threat—the only kind that matters to a European order that remains insulated from external threats by the implied U.S. security guarantee.

Furthermore, binding all member states and EU institutions to European law has created a new tradition and with it a new political reality. The protection of particular national interests of all member states now depends on a functioning EU. But while that means that a fundamental reconfiguration of Europe's integration process is almost inconceivable, its erosion is not. In fact, that would be precisely the consequence of the EU's failure to address its lack of democratic legitimacy and efficacy.

To sum up: on the one hand, the EU has been an enormous accomplishment. It has created an unparalleled, stable state of security for all of Europe, a common market, and a common currency. It has added a total of fifteen member states since 1989, expanded freedom of movement by removing internal borders, and at least begun to craft a common foreign and security policy with joint international EU civil and military missions. Against the backdrop of European history, such achievements reaffirm the idea of progress.

On the other hand, over the past two decades, Europeans have shown a consistent inability to adapt their common institutions to the demands of enlargement and to a world that is undergoing rapid and radical change. That reflects the failure of Europe's elites to foster the emotional support of citizens that is necessary for the common European project to succeed. Instead of generating democratic legitimacy for European integration, Europe's elites seem able to deliver only a chronic hardening of opposition to the project.

BIGGER AND BETTER

Institutional reform and democracy are intimately connected because an enlarged EU without effective institutions will become even more opaque and inefficient in the public eye, while opportunities for compromise within the European Council will be further reduced. And, from the perspective of Europe's peace and stability as well as its power, the importance of enlargement cannot be overestimated. By offering the prospect of membership (and lesser forms of association, with privileged market access), Europe wields real influence in a difficult neighborhood that includes not only Russia, Ukraine, the southern Caucasus, and Turkey but also the Middle East and North Africa.

Enlargement policy is based on the promise of full membership, along with extensive financial subsidies for candidate states that enact structural reforms and bring their economies into line with the practices of the common market. After accession to the EU, new member states enjoy full rights, including veto power over questions of treaty ratification and in areas that require unanimity. They also obtain generous structural subsidies to modernize their industries and infrastructure, not to mention the advantages of integration into the common market. The prerequisite for obtaining all these blessings is meeting the Copenhagen Criteria—that is, accepting and implementing the EU's core values and the *acquis communautaire* (the complete body of EU law).

The prospect of EU membership therefore offers nothing less than successful rejuvenation of a country's economy, society, government, and legal system. By projecting power in this way, the EU has pioneered a policy that recognizes that security in the twenty-first century must be founded not primarily on military dominance but on complete and transformative modernization as well as on the harmonization, and even integration, of national interests. The EU can be neatly summed up as a partial relinquishment of sovereignty for the sake of guaranteed modernization and stability.

But it is precisely the promise of enlargement—Europe's most important source of power—that is increasingly endangered by the EU's inability to enact institutional reform. Indeed, it is conceivable that the Irish "no" will continue to stall the Lisbon Treaty's ratification, which would leave the EU's enlargement policy in shambles because the union simply no longer has the institutional capacity to maintain its functions and efficiency while absorbing new states.

This is why the desire of Great Britain and other euroskeptics to enlarge the EU while preventing consolidation is illusory. As has been evident since 1989, enlargement without integration is undermining the EU's capacity to act. In a persistently precarious region—and in a realigned world order in which China, India, Brazil, Russia, and the United States are global players—this self-imposed weakness will strain the EU's inner cohesion and drastically reduce Europe's influence in the world.

THE EU IN THE FINANCIAL CRISIS

The global financial crisis has laid bare the European Union's flaws and limitations. Indeed, what Europe lost, first and foremost, with the rejection of the constitutional treaty is now obvious: its faith in itself and its common future. Amid this worst crisis since the Great Depression, each passing day seems to drive EU members further backward, toward the national egoism and protectionism of the past.

The euro and the European Central Bank (ECB) have been bulwarks in defending monetary stability during the financial crisis. Any weakening of those institutions would cause severe damage to common European interests, but the behavior of EU member governments during the past few months raises doubt about whether they recognize that fact. As the crisis continues, it becomes obvious that the common currency and the ECB alone are not sufficient to defend the common market and European integration. Without common economic and financial policies, coordinated at the very least among the members of the euro zone, the cohesion of the common currency too is in unprecedented danger. In Italy, Spain, Ireland, Portugal, and Greece, confidence is rapidly evaporating. Though the stronger economies in northern Europe are doing better, they too are struggling. Should that continue, perhaps bringing a de facto end to the Maastricht criteria and rising national protectionism in the form of industrial subsidies, the euro will be seriously jeopardized. It is easy to imagine what the euro's failure would mean for the EU as a whole: a disaster of historic proportions.

The new EU member states in eastern Europe, which have neither the economic strength nor the political stability of long-term members, are now beginning to take a nosedive. Given the exposure of some eurozone states such as Austria, this crisis will also affect the euro area directly. To wait and see is, therefore, the wrong strategy.

There is no reason to believe that the current global economic crisis has bottomed out. If it intensifies further, Europe will rapidly face a grim alternative: either the richer and more stable economies in the north—first and foremost Europe's largest economy, Germany—will use their greater financial resources to help the weaker euro-zone economies, or the euro will be endangered and with it the whole project of European integration. It must never be forgotten that the EU is a project designed for mutual economic progress. If that economic bond disappears, national interests will reassert themselves and rip the project apart.

SALVAGING EUROPE

So, what will the EU look like in 2030? If one looks back just twenty years from today, to 1989, there is little ground for optimism that the EU, with its existing structures, will make more than limited progress. It certainly will not become a world power. While it will not be threatened with collapse, it will be subject to steady erosion and decline, reflected in key indicators such as demographic growth, proportion of the world's population, and share of the global economy. That means that Europe will have to contend with a relative, but nevertheless dramatic, loss of power, for the EU's cohesion and appeal have, to a great extent, always been based on the promise of prosperity and growth. With that promise now threatened by macroeconomic and global political trends, the EU's internal erosion will accelerate.

Europe's relative decline will fan popular fears of globalization and diminish support for further EU enlargement. It will encourage populism, nationalism, and sharpening competition for increasingly scarce EU resources. In addition, there is the question of Germany, the largest and most economically powerful member state, which had previously tied its national interests to the EU but which, faced with the logjam of European integration, is already "renationalizing" its policy to support narrowly defined German interests, further weakening the union's cohesion.

Indeed, the Franco-German engine, which is crucial to the EU acting in unison, appears blocked, at least at the moment. Their rhetoric suggests that France and Germany have a great deal in common, but the facts tell a completely different story. In nearly all strategic aspects of EU crisis management, Germany and France are blocking each other—although ironically, both are doing virtually the same thing. They are thinking first and foremost of themselves, not of Europe, which is thus, in effect, without leadership.

The EU was and is an institutionalized compromise, and it must remain so now, in the midst of a global economic crisis. If Germany and France do not quickly resolve their differences and find a joint strategic answer to the crisis, they will damage themselves and Europe as a whole.

Even if the Lisbon Treaty were finally ratified, Europe would remain unable to act in concert for a significant time, since the EU-27 will be in no position to coordinate a common strategic plan. The respective national positions are simply too different, and most national governments lack incentives to bring Europe further along in a common project. That reflects the compromise struck by pro-Europeans and euroskeptics after 1989, which enabled enlargement but also contributed significantly to the loss of the European project's emotional and visionary qualities and reduced EU reforms to the lowest common denominator.

Now, even that compromise has finally been undone by Ireland. With the Irish "no" to the Lisbon Treaty, Europe has been thrown back on the reality of a two-speed integration process. Henceforth, if the erosion of Project Europe is to be stopped, European politics will once again be divided into an avant-garde and a rearguard.

It would be preferable if such a two-speed Europe were to function within the framework of the Lisbon Treaty—without which institutional reform is impossible—but the key point is that those states that want to continue along the path of integration, and can, should do so. The states that do not want to, or that cannot, continue along that path should remain behind rather than stall the others' progress. It would be better to proceed divided than to remain at a standstill together—and thus better to live with a system of extensive opt-outs than with persistent logjams. Only in that manner can the next two decades rekindle a new dynamism in favor of European integration. Reclaiming European citizens' confidence and support requires addressing foreign and defense policy, financial and economic policy, energy policy, and the organization of Europe's social-welfare arrangements. And here, a group of states can lead the way decisively, regardless of whether they do so within or outside of the treaties.

With an even tighter federation, deeper integration, more efficient and transparent institutions, a greater democratic consensus, and a strategic expansion that admits Turkey, Europe could stop its dramatic relative decline by 2030 and even reverse it. A boost in terms of European solidarity and legitimacy—that is, the emotional cohesion of Europe's citizens—could provide a decisive counterweight to the growing centrifugal forces within the EU. Yet those very attributes are in scarce supply after the Dutch, French, and Irish referendums.

That is why I doubt that Europe's malaise can be overcome before 2030. The current situation, combined with the dramatic lack of leadership in today's generation of European politicians, militates against a positive outcome, much less a strong, united Europe. Indeed, there will be hardly anything that one could call a European government. While the partial creation of a common defense system, along with a European army, is possible by 2030, a common foreign policy is not. Expansion of the EU to include the Balkan states, Turkey, and Ukraine should also be ruled out.

Constrained by dysfunctional institutions and diminishing effectiveness, Europe as a world power and global partner of the United States will, for an indeterminate period, be capable of only limited action on the international stage. That is not good news for those who believe that the West as a strategic reality continues to be indispensable to a global future of freedom, prosperity, and security. At some point, crises and acute threats may force the Europeans to grow up quickly. Despite the financial crisis, Europe today does not lack economic strength, but rather the political will to act in unison. Unfortunately, from today's perspective, almost everything argues against Europe's emergence as a world power; instead, it remains a hamster on a wheel—constantly in motion, but never making any progress.

2

The Limits of the European Union in 2030: A Best-Case Scenario

A week is a long time in politics.
—Harold Wilson (1916–95), British prime minister, 1964–70 and 1974–76

Ce qui m'étonne, dit Dieu, c'est l'espérance.
—Charles Péguy (1873–1914), French poet killed in action by the Germans

IN 2030 the European Union remained an open-ended venture. On successive occasions between the end of the twentieth century and the middle of the second decade of the twenty-first, a few concerned politicians, mostly in France and Germany, had raised the issue of what they called the borders of Europe, which they thought should be unmistakably defined and set in stone to preserve the cultural identity of the Union and keep the barbarians at the gate. But no serious public debate on the matter ever took place in any member state, and each attempt eventually petered out, leaving the Union as borderless as before.

To wit, after the great enlargement of 2004 brought in Poland and nine small and medium-sized states that were said to be teeming with men and women ready to flood the old Union's labor market, concern was widely

Translation of Péguy quote: "What astonishes me, says God, is hope."

voiced about "absorption capacity"—a dubious term of difficult objective measurement that was, at bottom, a barely disguised Christian aversion to Turkey's accession. According to those concerned, although no wall should be built around the Union, which remained theoretically open to any properly qualified candidate, the pace of further enlargement should be deliberately slowed because experience had shown that the peoples of Europe needed time to prepare for the arrival of more newcomers. Despite populist onslaughts, however, the push to close the Union made no headway, perhaps because it flew against basic European interests. Those interests were well understood by business people and economists, who had long hoped for continuing growth because a shrinking and aging European population was in need of fresh young blood to compete in the world market and decently pension off its elderly. Subsequent enlargements, therefore, continued to be negotiated at their own pace. And an article added to the French Constitution by President Jacques Chirac requiring popular referenda to ratify new accessions to the Union—in fact another attempt at keeping Turkey out—was eventually dropped a few years later. By 2030 the gate remained unlocked and barbarians were still knocking at it, albeit fewer than there had been twenty years before.

Of course, in 2030, as in 2008, the European Union had geographical limits, which ran along the outer borders of its peripheral member states and established a barrier against would-be migrants, some of whom were kept out although many were let in, usually under strict regulations. In 2000 the United Nations had estimated that the EU would need 159 million outside workers by 2025; in 2030 that number had not been reached. There were, however, no EU borders demarcating Europe's final boundaries.

The widespread understanding of basic European interests that stood behind the EU's openness to new members had been strongly stimulated by two different sets of considerations. The first was that enlargement—starting with the first one in 1973, which brought in Britain, Ireland, and Denmark—had always boosted European vigor, which during the first quarter of the twenty-first century was needed more than ever, because globalization was increasing international competition far beyond earlier expectations. Popular awareness that Europe was a more vigorous entity than it had been during the cold war—although militarily the Europeans were weaker than they had been at any time for the last five hundred years—took some time to sink in. But a succession of challenges—perhaps more than anything else the need to cope with energy scarcity and to parry perceived provocations by Russia—eventually helped clear the minds of many Europeans on that score. The second, related reason was, at least on the surface, a paradox: the European Union had not become a political global actor despite the hopes of some of its most idealistic and eloquent champions. Although it registered growing commercial, economic, and regulatory successes—illustrated, for instance, by the record fine imposed on Gazprom by the European Commission in 2015, exceeding those imposed on Microsoft in 2004 and 2008—and Western-inspired democracy and rule of law began their slow but steady spread to governments in other parts of the world, the EU's fuzzy and unwieldy political nature had not changed. It was no more of a federation of states, let alone a superstate, than it had been almost two decades earlier. Talk of a political "ever closer union," which had first been heralded in the preamble of the 1957 Treaty of Rome and was a central ambition in the rhetoric of continental statesmen for three generations, had practically vanished from European political discourse by 2030.

Accordingly, European foreign, security, and defense policies had not developed much further. Despite the Union External Service, which was led by a quasi–foreign minister, the bulk of European traditional diplomatic transactions continued to be conducted at the national level, particularly when the issues were important to the country concerned. The new EU "embassies" started by doing the type of work that had been done before by the European Commission delegations—which looked like an uneasy mix of humanitarian NGO branches and trade offices—and then widened their scope as energy and immigration policies became more communitarian than national. From the onset, in this or that third country, consular services had conveniently been offered to members with no diplomatic representation there, and little by little other traditional diplomatic chores were transferred from member states (particularly the small ones) to the Union. Foreign trade and foreign policy developed better awareness of each other. Attempts were made to give political guidance or at least some coherence to development aid. In the early years, Poland and the Baltic states had hoped that the reinforced Common Foreign and Security Policy would help them to use the EU's clout against

Russia, but that happened only on exceptional occasions; most of the time, when relations with Russia or other controversial questions arose, they had either toed the Union line or, more often than not, went their separate ways because there was no Union line to toe. As expected, France and the United Kingdom had kept their permanent seats at the Security Council, and the Union as such had not gained one. By 2030 the Common Foreign and Security Policy remained largely "à la carte."

In military affairs, the lofty Gaullist vision of "l'Europe de la défense" had been dealt a blow by a direct political heir of the general's, having been "realistically adapted to the twenty-first century," as French officials liked to put it in President Nicolas Sarkozy's day. In other words, France concentrated on reinforcing the EU's link with the United States instead of on weakening it. NATO, which nimbly survived radical changes in threats and in strategy, remained the bedrock of Western security, with most EU members being Atlantic allies too. When it came to other aspects of security, notably crisis management—trying to sort out other peoples' troubles in order to safeguard European interests, mostly in Africa—the EU had found itself a niche. At least that was the rule so long as the troubles to be addressed were not unduly large, in which case the only suitable military toolbox had to be found in NATO. The 1999 European Council vow to be able to deploy 60,000 men to a faraway place for six months was not realized by the promised deadline of 2003 or any later date. In short, the European Union remained a military worm and a political dwarf, as a Belgian prime minister had once said.

But it remained an economic giant—and more. Outside those political and military matters that had always been dealt with intergovernmentally, the EU's strength and influence had been considerably enhanced by what Europeans had learnt to do in common. The range of matters treated by the so-called "communitarian method" had widened. Between 2008 and 2030, immigration (dealt with by the European Commission, along with international crime, under the heading Liberty, Justice, and Security) as well as energy (including the import, storage, and transport of gas and oil) had been added to agriculture, the internal market, competition, external trade, and the euro, which was being independently run by the European Central Bank. In fact, the EU derived a considerable part of its increased strength as an international player from the establishment of a common energy policy, which, although it had been very difficult to establish, was up and running by 2020. With the exception of Germany—and even Germany, as the years passed by, regained some imperial traits that other big powers had never lost—the large European countries bore an ingrained hostility to the communitarian method because it forced them to take into account the views of small and medium-sized countries in a manner to which they were not accustomed. (De Gaulle liked to call the European Community "*le machin*"; he said of the European project that nations were hard-boiled eggs and with hard-boiled eggs one could not make an omelette.)

Moreover, in the case of energy, several member states, large and small, had been lured by Russia to enter bilateral supply arrangements, which later had had to be renegotiated to comply with the new Common Energy Policy. The German case was especially difficult to sort out because large joint steps had been undertaken by Berlin and Moscow from the days of Chancellor Gerhard Schröder and President Vladimir Putin and because economic relations between the two countries were so wide-ranging and deeply rooted. It took years of hard bargaining and meticulous disentanglement—helped by occasional Russian clumsiness and the opportunity offered by the Ukrainian partition of 2018—for the EU to be able to import Russian gas and oil as a single consumer and to subject Gazprom to the discipline of European competition policy. That ultimately reinforced the Union's negotiating position in energy deals to an extent that far exceeded what any individual member state could have achieved on its own. That strengthened the EU in other areas of international trade too, giving Europeans a more comfortable position in the world than they had ever enjoyed in the past. A single market of 650 million people went a long way—longer, certainly, than the triumphant national armies of yore.

In an era when cohesion funds had long disappeared from the EU's budget and the Common Agricultural Policy had been divested of its protectionist elements, the Union did not always speak with a single political voice on important international issues. There was, as noted, no European military power to speak of. Still, what kept national governments, parliaments, and peoples keen on sticking with the European vessel—and what gave that vessel its geopolitical clout—were first and foremost the considerable advantages that membership gave countries in the globalized market for goods, services, labor, and money and, last but not least, European civic and political values.

In 2030 the EU was also stronger for having resisted two centrifugal pulls, one internal and the other external. Internally, Lisbon Treaty innovations introduced after the second Irish referendum in 2009 reinforced the power of the big member states, which gained stronger voting rights in the European Council at the expense of the medium-sized and small ones. The trimming of the semiannual rotating presidencies deprived prime ministers and foreign ministers of six months of a highly visible performance on the European stage. Although the European Commission continued to keep one member from each country at all times, the sense of ownership of the European process by European citizens from large and small countries alike was enfeebled. As a result, a certain European "esprit de corps" was bruised. Interaction between national governments and EU bodies as well as among national governments themselves became somewhat rough. In the nationalist mood of the 2010s and 2020s, patriotic feathers were easily ruffled, and at times the future of the whole European enterprise seemed uncertain.

Externally, the workings of business and communications in the new global marketplace allowed for the kind of success that might have tempted some member states to go their own way as fully independent states unfettered by the limits on sovereignty imposed by membership. The Lisbon Treaty had given member states the right to leave the Union, and Norway and Switzerland had shown that European countries could live prosperously and comfortably outside the EU. But in a world in which self-aggrandizing optimism had lost its power of persuasion, two long-term factors steadied the EU: the material satisfaction of the populations of member states and the fact that the European experiment in peace and democracy was being tried in other parts of the world, easing international trade and making wars less likely.

So the two centrifugal pulls that might have lured countries away from the European project did not add up in the end. Between 2008 and 2030 no member state left, probably because each government and people, from the smallest to the largest, preferred the benefits of the Union to the likely gains of faring for themselves in the Brave New World. That was especially felt through the world's financial meltdown and economic crisis of 2008–10. For the same reasons, candidate countries kept knocking at the EU's door.

The original twenty-seven signatory states of the 2007 Lisbon Treaty became twenty-eight when Scotland split from the United Kingdom in 2014 without leaving the European Union. Between 2011 and 2020 the former Yugoslav republics of Croatia, Serbia, Bosnia-Herzegovina, and Montenegro had joined the Union, along with the Republic of Albania, which embraced Kosovo in a self-proclaimed "Greater Albania Confederation" to which only Germany, Austria, and Croatia extended acceptance (though of an informal sort comparable to that given to Taiwan by countries that did not want to harm their diplomatic relations with China). Kosovo on its own could not join because it remained unrecognized by a number of EU countries, and Macedonia had been kept at the door by insurmountable Greek objections concerning its name, first raised in 1991 when the Federal Republic of Yugoslavia was dissolved. Except for those two small, landlocked patches, the whole of the western Balkans was now part of the EU.

After a lengthy and bumpy accession process, Turkey joined in 2023, sixty years after signing its first association agreement with the European Community. For more than fifty of those years—both before and after the end of the cold war—Turkey's European ambitions had not been at the forefront of European preoccupations, but then the mood changed. The announcement of the opening of accession negotiations between Turkey and the European Union in 2005 aroused European public opinion, which was sharply divided on the issue. Spurred by eloquent politicians from both sides, the debate on Turkey's accession seemed at times to suggest that Turkey would never join the club, although Greece, the United Kingdom, and Sweden, among others, were determinedly pro-Turkish. The case of Greece was especially instructive: because of historical differences and much bad blood, Greeks had long opposed the idea of accepting Turkey in the European Union. Eventually, however, it dawned on the Greeks that if Turkey did not become the EU's southeastern buffer, that dubious privilege would fall on Greece. By contrast, Germany remained divided down the middle for many years: Social Democrats were for and Christian Democrats against. The French right was vociferously against, particularly during the Sarkozy presidency.

In Turkey itself, opinion was divided as well, and it reacted to fluctuations in European opinion. Each sign of rejection from European politicians—usually grounded in the "Turkey is not part of Europe" geographical argument that Helmut Kohl had put forward or in the more naked anti-Muslim bias of "alleged unbridgeable cultural differences"—gave renewed strength to anti-European Turks. They included both secular nationalists, who favored close arrangements with the EU short of membership that would confer economic advantages without burdensome human rights obligations, and Islamic fundamentalists for whom the moderate pragmatism of the pro-European Justice and Development (AKP) party had become anathema.

Despite three failed attempts at "judicial coups d'état" (in 2008, 2013, and 2017) by the Constitutional Court in Ankara, Turkey enjoyed remarkable political stability between 2005 and 2023, from the opening of accession negotiations to the actual accession. During that period, the military, which throughout the history of the republic had considered itself the guardian of Ataturk's secularist heritage, stopped meddling in politics altogether. Occasionally, for a few years after 2005, military officials had to be warned by Brussels and Washington against any attempt at unconstitutional interventions that would harm the chances of Turkey's accession to the EU and thus hinder the very westernization that the military wished the country to undergo. But in time, such warnings ceased to be needed. The High Command understood that the European Union helped to fulfil Mustapha Kemal's ambition of making Turkey a modern European power in ways more acceptable to modern sensibilities than their Anatolian *manu militare*. Moreover, the EU's pervasive influence helped reduce tensions over the vexed question of religion in Turkey by fostering, in the words of a well-known Turkish-Kurdish writer, a more tolerant "humanistic secularism" than had been the ideology of the armed forces, judiciary, and civil service. Besides, the new, less stressful political environment allowed the military to put its own house in order. Tempted by extreme forms of Islam, restive young officers occasionally strayed from the secular path and had to be brought in line. That could be done now with much less risk of raising national tensions: in fact, the Islamists in power in Ankara (and Istanbul)—*mutatis mutandis* Christian Democrats of the Muslim faith—tacitly welcomed the general staff's house cleaning. In short, as it gained pace, the process of European accession was convenient to almost everybody.

A variety of realizations led to the European change of heart that eventually allowed for Turkish accession. The prospect of a permanent infusion of much-needed labor and of the reinforcement of the EU's military strength became more tempting as Europeans continued to age and as Middle Eastern and Central Asian instability remained a source of security challenges. According to Eurobarometer opinion polls, another decisive reason was the growing public awareness of the role that Turkey could play in securing Europe's energy supply. Pipelines through Turkish territory could substantially reduce EU countries' dependence on Russian gas and oil.

That had been known for some time, but the issue moved to the center of attention at the end of the first decade of the century, when the price of oil jumped again during the recovery from the most serious Western financial crisis since 1929. Europeans felt besieged and weak. Their initial reactions had strong nationalist overtones and colorful echoes of class struggle. Soon, however, governments, businesses, and trade unions started working together across national borders. Increasing coordination between governments, the European Commission, and industry eventually led to the search for collective strategies to deal with the new problems. After some time, it became obvious to the EU's political classes that when it came to energy, the invaluable help available through Turkish cooperation was best secured if Turkey's membership ambitions were not constantly opposed or even procedurally thwarted by this or that European government. In France and Austria the realization of the "Turkish advantage," as some called it, was slower to arrive than elsewhere, but even there once strident anti-Turkish voices ceased to be heard and politicians from right and left started to preach the benefits of having Turkey in the Union—though some cast it as the lesser of two evils. As is customary in democracies, public opinion followed suit.

The debate on Turkey was harsher in Germany, where the sharp divide between Christian Democrats and Social Democrats was complicated by the Russia factor. Transporting oil and gas to the Union through Turkey harmed Russian interests and therefore became an element of the general European discussion on a common energy policy, a discussion in which Berlin was often reluctant to appear hostile to Russia or to endanger

German economic arrangements that had been negotiated bilaterally with Moscow. However, even Germany—where the debate was further roiled by ethnic tensions in working-class neighborhoods, mixed marriages, and religious prejudices—came down on the Turkish side in the end.

Thus, by 2030 the southeastern border of the European Union had been relocated by Turkey's accession. As in 2008, the EU was bordered on the south by the Mediterranean, on the west by the Atlantic Ocean, and on the north by the North Sea, Norway, and Russia. To the east, though, there had been another significant change. In 2020 Ukraine—or rather a bit more than half of it—was admitted to the European Union and to NATO. The Crimea, reversing Khruschev's 1954 gift of its territory to Ukraine, and other Russian-speaking regions in the eastern part of the country opted out of the European accession negotiations early on and voted to join the Russian Federation.

That the breakup of Ukraine took place without bloodshed or a dangerous political tug of war was not as surprising as it would have been a couple of decades earlier. Despite the number of linguistic groups and distinct historical traditions that coexisted within its borders, Ukraine's remarkable social stability had been severely tested by Russia's increasing reluctance to accept Crimea's status as final. The growing disagreement between the Russian-speaking and the Ukrainian-speaking majorities in the east and the west of the country on how to deal with the European Union and NATO added to the tension. That divide had been the main factor—contributing more than economic difficulties, including corruption—in the country's inability to form lasting governments since the 2004 Orange Revolution.

In 2015, after yet another hung parliament, leaders of the two sides started meeting secretly in Kiev to explore new ways to get Ukraine out of its rut. When they reached agreement, the country split from the top down. The precise drawing of the new border did not initially please everybody (after all, St. Vladimir had baptized the Russians in Kiev and Kiev remained in Ukraine), but it was accepted. There was a historical precedent, of a sort: in 1991 the Soviet Union also had folded top down in a peaceful manner—a welcome contrast to the disintegration of the Yugoslav Federation in the early 1990s. External circumstances had been propitious. The long protracted confrontation between the European Union and Russia that had accompanied the successful establishment of the European Common Energy Policy (CEP) had taught both sides how to deal better with one another in negotiations and nurtured a preference for mutually acceptable solutions. True, Russia had been unable to block the emergence of CEP, but in the end Moscow had come out of the ordeal with considerable practical advantages and, more important, a sense of being respected.

By 2030 Georgia and Moldova had not joined the European Union, although both had repeatedly expressed their strong interest in doing so. Neither had any of the other Caucasian republics that had once belonged to the Soviet Union; all were far too unstable and fractious for admission. To the southeast of Turkey there were neither candidates nor aspirants to candidacy. Norway in the north kept comfortably out, as did Switzerland in the middle. South of the Mediterranean, the EU door remained closed: the Union for the Mediterranean invented at French insistence in 2008 to improve on the so-called Barcelona Process had not bettered the chances of its southern shore members of making it to Brussels. Within its limitations, the old Neighborhood Policy delivered some prosperity and a modicum of political openness to a few North African, Near Eastern, and Caucasian countries. Thus, without grand declarations of geopolitical vision, it was as if the borders of the Union that Europeans needed to feel secure had been found after all.

Of course, in theory the European venture remained open, and perhaps those who assess the Union in 2050 will find that it covers more lands in a wider space—or perhaps not. Between 2008 and 2030, international circumstances were especially propitious for the peaceful development of Europe. After a bubble before 2010, oil prices had set at reasonable levels. The fright created by the bubble had prompted people to adopt better patterns of consumption and to make wiser investments in new sources of energy. Food prices came down too—though not to their previous low levels—as the West adapted to the fact that in many parts of the third world people had become accustomed to eating three meals a day. Like the oil industry, the agricultural industry all over the world, including in the traditionally protected Japanese, U.S., and European markets, learned and improved. Global warming did not hit the world like a tsunami. In fact, as some wise scientists had predicted, its advances were slow and uneven, although a loud, sanctimonious choir had made that prediction difficult to hear. From the poles to the tropics, changes in nature, man-made or otherwise, were manageable over the previous two decades. Finally, the growth and expansion of the new great competitors in world trade, influence, and power—particularly China and India— also proved to be less fearsome than had been predicted by many in the West. Internal inequalities and the relentless social aspirations of their populations consistently put too much on the plates of their rulers to incline them to external adventures. Both nations saw advantages in smoothing relations with the United States and Europe.

Finally, in a globalized world, the Europeans benefited from the spread of their vaunted political values and habits, which historians, political scientists, and so-called opinion makers of the realist persuasion had long thought unlikely. Slowly but steadily, parliamentary democracy, the rule of law, and separation of powers, together with some protection of human rights, were grafted here and there into the constitutions of more countries in other parts of the world, regardless of cultural tradition and religious persuasion. Not all the experiments had immediate good results, but many did: in Africa, despite a contrarian Chinese onslaught early in the century, and in Asia and in Latin America, where a growing adjustment of the existing political traditions to those of post–World War II democratic Europe nurtured some decency in relations between governments and the governed and contributed to making international life a little less prone to war. While that lasted—and it had lasted until 2030—it suited the European Union. Against all odds—first in the cocoon spun by the nuclear confrontation between the United States and the USSR and then in the often bewildering aftermath of the cold war—Europe had spent half a century unwittingly preparing itself, to paraphrase Kant, for perpetual peace and perpetual decency.

JOSEPH H. H. WEILER 3

The Accidental Constitution

THE AFTERMATH OF A bitter divorce may not seem to be the most auspicious time for reflecting on the future of matrimony. In the light of the dramatic failure of the European Constitution and the exorcism from its successor, the Treaty of Lisbon, of any "constitutional" vocabulary or iconography, this may appear to be an inauspicious time to try to imagine the constitutional future of Europe twenty years from now. It would seem that neither the EU's institutions and member states nor "The People(s)" are in a constitutional mood. What impact will these events have on the prospects for a European constitution?

It is not clear how deep and lasting the wounds of rejection may be or whether a reversal of fortune is in the cards. Who today, for example, remembers the Draft Constitution prepared by the European Parliament in the early 1990s in the follow-up to the Maastricht Treaty? Even its own promoters were quick to consign it to oblivion since, at that time, it spelt political death. To speak of a constitution for Europe was to be tainted with the "F word"—to be branded an old-fashioned federalist. Talk of a constitution seemed to be dead forever.

And yet, a mere ten years later, there emerged a political and intellectual stampede to embrace the idea of a constitution for Europe. Joschka and Jacques and Valéry and Helmut all waded in and gave the idea political respectability.[1] Habermas "koshered the reptile" in intellectual circles.[2] Though the Convention on the Future of Europe was not officially a constitutional convention, it was dubbed the European Philadelphia by its very president.

At first it seemed as if "the people" too were swept by the rhetoric. Spain was said in the press to have given a "gift" to Europe with its popular approval of the "Constitution." In hindsight, the scrutiny that Spain applied to the proposition does not look quite so laudable. Indeed, as an exercise in European civic culture, it was symptomatic of a growing trend of public indifference and apathy exemplified by the shockingly low turnout for the referendum and the debased quality of public discourse.

In 2005, the spirited and healthy public debates that took place in France and the Netherlands—and the decisive rejection of the "Constitution" by the people of those two founding members—dealt a seemingly fatal blow to the project. The precise reasons for the rejection of the "Constitution" itself and the subsequent Irish rejection of the Lisbon Treaty—as well as the subsequent turnabout—will never be known. But, normatively speaking, those rejections should come as no surprise. By way of explanation, let me start with a famous example of Jewish humor:

> Moishe and Chayim, two fur traders, meet at Warsaw Railway Station. "Where are you going to?" asks Moishe. "To Lodz," answers Chayim. "Oy, you are so dishonest!" says Moishe. "You tell me you are going to Lodz because you want me to think that you are going to Krakow. But actually you are really going to Lodz! So why are you fibbing?"

Begin to wrap your mind around the subtle and multiple layers of deception encapsulated in that little exchange. Now imagine a variant: Moishe says:

> You tell me you are going to Lodz because you want me to think that you want me to think that you are going to Krakow and that I will therefore think that you are actually going to Lodz but you are in fact going to Krakow.

Reach for your bottle of aspirin. Now we are in the right frame of mind to uncover the multiple layers of deception in the recent European constitutional saga.

The original sin was to confuse the institutional with the constitutional and to peddle the idea that Europe was in need of a formal constitution. What it really needed was a serious institutional face lift, updating its decisionmaking processes to accommodate a union of twenty-seven members. Constitutionally, Europe was doing just fine, notably in the critical area of the relationship between the European Union, the member states, and European citizens. Not only had that relationship historically followed a constitutional rather than an international law sensibility and discipline, it was original and noble. The member states accepted the supremacy of European Union law, individuals could rely on their European rights even in the face of conflicting state norms, and the European Court of Justice developed a robust doctrine of protection of fundamental human rights—long before anyone even thought about the Charter. The second deception was to pretend that the legal mongrel produced by the Convention on the Future of Europe was a constitution.

It did not look like a constitution. The English version came in at 154,183 words—in comparison, the U.S. Constitution is 5,800 words long and the Charter of the United Nations is 8,890—and the actual weight of the official two-tome printed version is just under one kilogram.

It did not read like a constitution. Constitutional preambles typically are of a magisterial style and make reference to the ultimate constitutional authority undergirding the document—the People. Thus, for example (italics added):

> We *the people of the United States*, in order to form a more perfect union . . .

> *Le peuple français* proclame solennellement son attachement aux Droits de l'homme et aux principes de la souveraineté nationale tels qu'ils ont été définis par la Déclaration de 1789 . . .

> Im Bewußtsein seiner Verantwortung vor Gott und den Menschen, von dem Willen beseelt, als gleichberechtigtes Glied in einem vereinten Europa dem Frieden der Welt zu dienen, hat sich *das Deutsche Volk* kraft seiner verfassungsgebenden Gewalt dieses Grundgesetz gegeben . . .

The opening phrase of the document put before Europe's peoples was equally revealing. It was the very same used since the first treaty establishing the European Coal and Steel Community in 1951—"His Majesty the King of the Belgians"—followed by a long list of heads of state:

> The President of the Czech Republic, Her Majesty the Queen of Denmark, the President of the Federal Republic of Germany [and so forth] have designated as their plenipotentiaries . . . Guy Verhofstadt Prime Minister[,] Karel de Gucht Minister for Foreign Affairs [and so forth], who, having exchanged their full powers, found in good and due form, have agreed as follows . . .

Non-initiated readers would be forgiven if they believed that they were reading the standard opening of an international treaty. They also would be forgiven if they formed the same opinion by going to the conclusion of the document, where they would first find this:

> This Treaty shall be ratified by the High Contracting Parties in accordance with their respective constitutional requirements. The instruments of ratification shall be deposited with the Government of the Italian Republic.

Followed by this:

> IN WITNESS WHEREOF, the undersigned plenipotentiaries have signed this Treaty

Res ipsa loquitur! And what of the content of the document, its substance? It was for the most part, including the integration of the Charter of Fundamental Rights, the kind of content that one had hoped to see in the Treaty of Amsterdam and certainly in the Treaty of Nice. It included a sensible though far from radical amendment of the institutional architecture and decisionmaking processes of the European Union, some meaningful but equally nonradical nods toward the further democratization of the Union, the European Charter, and some sensible cleaning up of language. The treaty revision procedures were amended to create a multi-tier process: convention and intergovernmental process; intergovernmental process without convention; decision of the European Council alone. But all three processes are, according to conventional thinking, typical not of constitutions but of treaties. They all require unanimity among the governments of the high contracting parties and ratification by national procedures in all member states.

Europe paid a heavy price by this double deception. Had it been presented for what it really was rather than under its misleading characterization as a constitution (based on the earlier deception that a constitution was needed), the peoples of Europe in their wisdom would have most likely welcomed it for what it really was: a reform treaty adapting the European Union to enlargement. No one would have used any superlatives to describe its content; it would have attracted very limited public attention or debate in most member states; it certainly would not have generated the numerous referenda that followed; and there would have been no talk of the need for a constitution—except, perhaps, among the extreme European federalist fringe. No Convention on the Future of Europe, no European Philadelphia, no Constitutionspeak. And Europe would have found itself with a sensible reform treaty a lot earlier and with no trauma.

Instead, once the document was presented as a constitution, it was only natural that a different standard of scrutiny be applied. A constitution, after all, is a document with far greater gravitas. In a constitution, one wants to find not simply sensible reform but a statement of identity, of ideals, of the type of society and polity that one not only is but wants to believe that one is. And against that appropriate standard, the mongrel document, the treaty masquerading as a constitution, which found favor with bureaucrats, eurocrats, and government ministers, was found wanting by the peoples of Europe and, ultimately, rejected.

In the latest macabre twist, the pretend constitution was repackaged with a new name—the Treaty of Lisbon, or the Reform Treaty. The repackaging was pretty crude. The word "constitution" had been stripped out. The Charter of Fundamental Rights is formally not part of the Reform Treaty, but it has been integrated, through a small legal provision, through the back door. So legally it is included, but in terms of presentation, it has been airbrushed out—and all this done whilst the repackagers were pontificating on the need for transparency.

With a few words stripped away but its substance largely intact, what's left of the former "Constitution" has been presented as a reform treaty, whereas it is really the very same constitution that was rejected last year, which really was a reform treaty pretending to be a constitution. Even Moishe now would need a bottle of aspirin.

Cleverly, the powers that be avoided as far as possible plebiscites for the approval of the Lisbon Treaty, and those who opposed were asked to think again and vote again or else. But in the light of this tale of mendacity and disillusion, the future of the European Constitution becomes, paradoxically, its past. The damage created by this moment of hubris in the history of European integration is not negligible.

First, there is the degradation of the political process and of the seriousness of civic discourse. Europe had officially adopted an Orwellian eurospeak in what was meant to be an upgrading of its legitimacy and transparency.

Second, there is damage to the future, since the "Non-Constitution" now defines the "promised land of European constitutionalism." Imagine reopening the debate on a European constitution in five or ten years. Imagine a text such as the one now abandoned, which still leaves an amending process that depends on the unanimous support of member states. By all accounts it should be objected to as contrary to a real constitution. But, with the legacy now created, we will hear that it is indeed acceptable—after all, didn't the European Constitution of 2004 provide exactly for such unanimity? At a more profound level, our constitutional vocabulary has been diminished—inflationized.

Third, there will also be damage to the present. It would be nice to think that with the Lisbon Treaty one could just revert to the constitutional status quo ante. It will not be so easy. For example, the EU Constitution included, unnecessarily, a supremacy clause. So, something that was firmly established in the European constitutional architecture has been undermined—politically, not legally—and will be challenged sooner or later. Let me make clear: Legally, we are where we were. But politically, the damage has been done. The European Court, on more than one occasion, referred to the EU Treaties as the Constitutional Charter of Europe. And the member states and their constitutional organs—parliaments, courts, and executive branches—were invited to submit to a "new legal order," which was constitutional in nature and defined the originality and nobility of the European construct. Could that important vocabulary be restored in the face of the rejection of the formal constitution?

Finally, the irony of the recent castigation of Ireland is no less damaging. In the ambition and desire to make constitutional progress, Chancellor Merkel was quite happy to threaten the most unconstitutional of moves, to ride roughshod over the requirement of unanimity for treaty amendment. And Nicolas Sarkozy was only slightly less blunt. What confidence is there in constitutional integrity if the champions of the Constitution are willing to violate the most primordial tenets of constitutional law when things do not go their way?

FORWARD TO THE PAST: EUROPE'S EXTANT CONSTITUTIONALISM

The very advent of the constitution saga, with its obsession with the future of Europe, demonstrated the deep failure of Europe's contemporary leadership to understand its present. The general view is that the constitutional failure of the present will be forgotten, giving Europe a second, or third, chance at meaningful constitution making. The central thesis of this essay, however, is that the present or the constitutional status quo represents the real promised land of Europe and that the attempts to fix that which is not only functional, but original and even noble, represent not progress but regress.

Let us first understand the sense of that claim and then speculate about future scenarios of Europe 2030. To that end, I will use the common trope of situating Europe within a comparative federal framework.[3]

The History of the Present: Europe's Fateful Choice

In the vision of the great thinker and teacher of federalism, the late Dan Elazar, Europe is already federalist. The federal principle, he explained, should not be confused with its specific manifestation in the federal state.[4] Echoing the same thought, Pescatore, the John Marshall of European Law, has observed that

> the methods of federalism are not only a means of organising states. . . . [F]ederalism is a political and legal philosophy which adapts itself to all political contexts on both the municipal and the international level, wherever and whenever two basic prerequisites are fulfilled: the search for unity, combined with genuine respect for the autonomy and the legitimate interests of the participant entities.[5]

It is therefore not surprising that comparisons between the distinct federalisms in North America and Europe have constituted a staple feature in the ongoing discussion concerning European integration.[6] Institutional arrangements have attracted a great deal of attention because of the apparent divergence of the European experience from the typical federation. In contrast with the classical model of the federal state and despite considerable refinements, Europe's institutional structure still adheres to the original supranational design of commission–council–parliament and continues to guarantee a decisive voice in European governance to the governments of the member states. The formal empowerment of the European Parliament over the years has been counterbalanced by informal empowerment of the Medusa-like European Council. Indeed, the institutional provisions of the defunct constitution and the extant Reform Treaty envisage a further strengthening of the intergovernmental voice by the selection of a president of the Council who will serve long term instead of the current six months and operate alongside the president of the Commission. For its part, the Commission has had to struggle to preserve its own weight in the decisionmaking process. Though superficially (and to some, optimistically) one could compare the Commission to a federal executive branch, the Council to a senate-type state chamber, and the Parliament to a popular chamber, the realities of an intergovernmental Europe are still forcefully in place. To use somewhat archaic language of statecraft, institutionally Europe is closer to the confederal than it is to the federal, and there are no plans afoot to change that. Indeed, it would appear that the Lisbon Treaty reinforced the intergovernmental element in the institutional balance.

Constitutional arrangements, by contrast, have attracted considerable attention in comparative analyses because of their apparent *convergence* with the experience of the federal state. Typically, federations allocate certain powers to federal institutions, and the policies and laws that emanate from the exercise of those powers are the supreme law of the land. They operate without the intermediary of local government, and, in case of conflict, they trump conflicting norms. Federal state constitutions always create a vertical hierarchy of a triple nature—a hierarchy of norms that, in turn, is rooted in a vertical hierarchy of normative authority that, in turn, is situated in a hierarchy of real power. Despite many original intentions, federations end up with a concentration of both constitutional and institutional power at the federal level.

As a result of a combination of express treaty provisions (such as those stipulating that certain types of Community legislation would be directly applicable),[7] foundational principles of international law (such as the general principle of supremacy of treaties over conflicting domestic law, even domestic constitutional law[8]), and interpretations of the European Court of Justice,[9] a set of constitutional norms regulating the relationship between the European Union and its member states (or the member states and their union) emerged that is very much like similar sets of norms in most federal states. There is an allocation of powers, which in the experience of most federal states has often not been respected. There is the principle of the law of the land (in the EU called Direct Effect), and there is the grand principle of supremacy.

But there remains one huge difference: Europe's constitutional principles, even if materially similar, are rooted in a framework that is altogether different. In federations, whether American or Australian, German or Canadian, the institutions of a federal state are situated in a constitutional framework that presupposes the existence of a "constitutional demos," that is, a single *pouvoir constituant* made of the citizens of the federation. And it is in the sovereignty and supreme authority of those citizens, as a constituent power, that the specific constitutional arrangement is rooted.

In Europe, that presupposition simply does not hold. Simply put, Europe's constitutional architecture has never been validated or legitimated by a formal process of constitutional adoption by the European people as a whole. As a result, the existing European constitutional discipline does not enjoy the same kind of authority found in federal states whose federalism is rooted in the classical constitutional order. It is a constitution that lacks some of the classical conditions of constitutionalism. There is a hierarchy of norms—Community norms trump conflicting member state norms, for example. But that hierarchy is not rooted in a hierarchy of normative authority or in a hierarchy of real power. Indeed, European federalism is constructed with a top-to-bottom hierarchy of norms, but with a bottom-to-top hierarchy of authority and real power.

One would think that that would result in perennial instability. But one of the virtues of the European construct is that it produces not only a constructive normative effect but also a surprisingly stable political polity. Member states of the European Union accept their constitutional discipline with far more equanimity than, say, Quebec. There are, surely, many reasons for that, but one of them is the peculiar constitutional arrangement of Europe.

The distinctiveness of that constitutional arrangement is not accidental. Originally, in a fateful and altogether welcome decision, Europe rejected the federal state model. In the most fundamental statement of its political aspiration, articulated in the first line of the preamble of the Treaty of Rome and reproduced ever since, the gathering nations of Europe proclaimed themselves "[d]etermined to lay the foundations for an ever closer Union of the *peoples* of Europe [emphasis added]." Thus, even in light of greater European integration, the distinct peoplehood of the individual member states was to remain intact. That stands in contrast with the theory of most—and the practice of all—federal states, which predicate the existence of one people. Likewise, with all the vicissitudes from Rome to Nice, the EU Treaties have not departed from their original blueprint—see, for example, Article 2 EC of the treaty in force, which states the aim of achieving "economic and social cohesion and solidarity among *Member States*" [emphasis added]. Neither one people, then, nor one state—federal or otherwise.

Europe was relaunched twice in recent times: In the mid-1980s the Single European Act introduced, almost by stealth, the most dramatic development in the institutional evolution of the community achieved by a treaty amendment: majority voting in most domains of the single market. In the 1990s Maastricht introduced the most important material development, an economic and monetary union encapsulated in the European Central Bank and the euro. Architecturally, the combination of a "confederal" institutional arrangement and a "federal" legal arrangement seemed for a time to mark Europe's *Sonderweg*. It appeared to enable Europe to square an especially vicious circle by achieving a veritably high level of material integration comparable only to that found in fully fledged federations while also maintaining—in contrast with the experience of all such federations—powerful and, some would argue, strengthened member states.[10]

With all the constitutional razzmatazz of the 2000s, very few dared to suggest a full-fledged institutional overhaul and the reconstruction of a federal-type government that enjoyed direct legitimacy derived from an all-European electorate.[11] Instead, the principal innovation was to try to root the constitutional arrangement in a formal document carrying the title of "Constitution." What drove that hearkening to a formal constitution, subsequently frustrated? It is essential to know that if one is to consider the constitutional future of Europe. Four factors seem to have driven the interest in a formal constitution rather than the preexisting "constitutional arrangement" based on the EU Treaties.

The first factor was political. It was widely assumed, correctly or otherwise, that the institutional arrangements of the Union would become dysfunctional in an enlarged body of, say, twenty-seven members. A major overhaul seemed necessary. In the same vein, some believed, incorrectly in my view, that the extant constitutional arrangements would not work. In particular, it was argued, the absence of a formal constitution left all important constitutional precepts of the Union at the mercy of the constitutional order of this or that member state, threatening the principles of uniformity of and equality before the law and impeding the orderly functioning of the polity. One was forever worried about what the constitutional court of the Germans, Italians, Spaniards, and so forth would have to say about this or that. A formal constitution enjoying the legitimacy of an all-European *pouvoir constituant* would, once and for all, settle that issue.

The second factor was "procedural." The process of adopting a constitution—the debate that it was supposed to generate, the alliances that it was supposed to form, the opposition that it might have created— would all, it was said, be healthy for the democratic and civic ethos and praxis of the polity.

The third factor was material. In one of its most celebrated cases in the early 1960s, the European Court of Justice described the Community as a "new legal order for the benefit of which the States have limited their sovereign rights, albeit in limited fields." There was (and still is) a widespread anxiety that those fields were limited no more. Indeed, not too long ago a prominent European scholar and judge of the European Court wrote that there "simply is no nucleus of sovereignty that the Member States can invoke, as such, against the Community."[12] A constitution was thought of as an appropriate way to limit the growth of Community competences.

Of greatest interest was the final normative and conceptual drive behind the discussion. Normatively, the Union's disturbing absence of formal constitutional legitimation—despite making heavy constitutional demands on its constituent members—was considered problematic. If, as is the case, the existing European constitutional framework demands constitutional obedience by and within all member states even when it conflicts with the constitutional norms of the member state, then, it is argued, that framework should be legitimated by a constitution that has the explicit consent of its subjects instead of the current pastiche—which, like Toby, just "growed."

Conceptually, the disquiet with the European constitutional arrangement must be understood against a European constitutional discourse. On the one hand, there were those who attempted to describe, define, and understand the European *Grundnorm*—the fundamental norm or source from which the authority of European constitutional discipline derives. The search for that holy grail underscored a vast majority of the academic literature theorizing on European constitutionalism.

Early "Europeanists" liked to argue that the *Grundnorm*, typically expressed in, say, the principle of supremacy of European law over national law in cases of conflict, had shifted to the "central" or "general" power—that is, to Europe. That view is less in fashion today and is contested by those who point out that, both in fact and in law, ultimate authority still rests in national constitutional orders that sanction supremacy, define its parameters, and typically place limitations on it.

According to the latter view the *Grundnorm* or source of constitutional authority would shift only if one were to take the existing constitutional precepts and enshrine them in a formal constitution adopted by a European constitutional demos—that is, the peoples of Europe acting on that occasion as one people.

My interest in this debate is neither that of the international relations expert or social scientist trying to explain or predict the course that European integration has taken or will take. I am, instead, mostly interested in the normative values of which the constitutional and political discourse is an expression. For if Europe is to return to its constitution-building mode some years from now, the same stakes will be in play yet again.

I want to stake, therefore, a normative claim and explain why in my view the unique brand of European constitutional federalism—the status quo—represents not only Europe's most original political asset but also its deepest set of values, why formalization of the Constitution would threaten that asset, and why that matters and will continue to matter in the future. Europe—in 2020, in 2030, and in 2040—will always face this dilemma if it seeks to shift the extant constitutional status quo radically.

The Principle of European Constitutional Tolerance: Theory and Practice

The reason that the questions of *ultimate* authority and constitutional *Grundnorm* seem so important is that we consider the integrity of our *national* constitutional orders not simply a matter of legal obedience and political power but also of moral commitment and identity. We perceive our national constitutions as doing more than simply structuring the respective powers of government and the relationships between public authority and individuals or between the state and other agents. Our constitutions are said to encapsulate our fundamental values and thereby to reflect our collective identity as a people, as a nation, as a state, as a Community, as a Union. When we are proud of and attached to our constitutions, we are so for these very reasons: they are about restricting power, not enlarging it; they protect fundamental rights of the individual; and they define a collective identity that does not make us feel queasy in the way that some forms of ethnic identity might. Thus, in the endless debates about the European Union's constitutional order, national courts have become in the last decade far more aggressive in their constitutional self-understanding. The case law is well known. National courts are no longer at the vanguard of the "new European legal order," bringing the rule of law to transnational relations and empowering, through European Union law, individuals vis-à-vis member state authority. Instead, they stand at the gate and defend national constitutions against illicit encroachment from Brussels. The recent decision of the German Federal Constitutional Court of June 2009 on the matter of the Lisbon Treaty is the high watershed of this trend. The national courts have received a sympathetic hearing, since they are perceived as protecting fundamental human rights as well as protecting national identity. To protect national sovereignty is passé; to protect national identity by insisting on constitutional specificity is à la mode.

It is argued, therefore, that to submit to the constitutional discipline of Europe without a proper constitution, which formally vests ultimate authority in Europe, not only contradicts an orderly understanding of legal hierarchy but also compromises the deep values and collective identity enshrined in the national constitution. Indeed, it is to challenge the idea of constitution itself. Miguel Maduro, one of the most brilliant of the new generation of European constitutional thinkers, gives eloquent expression to that concern:

> European integration not only challenges national constitutions . . . ; it challenges constitutional law itself. It assumes a constitution without a traditional political community defined and proposed by that constitution. . . . European integration also challenges the legal monopoly of States and the hierarchical organisation of the law (in which constitutional law is still conceived of as the "higher law").[13]

Is this challenge so threatening?

In part, it is. Modern liberal constitutions are, indeed, about limiting the power of government vis-à-vis the individual; they do articulate fundamental human rights in the best neo-Kantian tradition; they do reflect a notion of collective identity as a community of values, far less threatening than more organic definitions of collective identity. They are a reflection of our better part. But, like the moon, like much that is good in life, it has a dark side too.

The advocacy for a formal European constitution was not what it purports to be. It is not a call for "a" constitution. It is a call for a form of European constitution that is different from the constitutional architecture that we already have. And yet, the current constitutional architecture, which of course can be improved in many of its specifics, embodies one of Europe's most important constitutional innovations, the *principle of constitutional tolerance*. That principle, which is the normative hallmark of European federalism, must be examined both as a concept and as a praxis.

First, the concept. Historically, European integration has been one of the principal means by which to consolidate democracy within and among several of the member states with less-than-perfect historical democratic credentials. Therefore, for many, democracy is the ultimate objective of the European construct. That is fallacious. Democracy is not the end. Democracy, too, is a means, even if an indispensable means. The end is to try, and try again, to live a life of decency in the best manner dictated by our collective values. A democracy, when all is said and done, is as good or bad as the people who belong to it.

Europe was built on the ashes of World War II, which witnessed the most horrific alienation of those thought of as aliens. What we should be thinking about is not simply the prevention of such carnage; that's the easy part. Although events in the Balkans remind us that demons are still at large within the continent, such is unlikely ever to happen again in western Europe. More difficult is dealing at a deeper level with the source of the attitudes that gave rise to it. In the realm of the social, in the public square, the relationship to the alien is at the core of human decency. It is difficult to imagine something normatively more important to the human condition and to our multicultural societies.

There are, it seems to me, two basic human strategies for dealing with the alien that have played a decisive role in Western civilization. One strategy is to remove the boundaries: It is the spirit of "Come, be one of us." It is noble because it involves the elimination of prejudice and the notion that all boundaries can be eradicated. But, however well intentioned, it often is also an invitation to become one of us by being us, and it risks robbing the alien of his or her identity. If I cannot tolerate the alien, one way of resolving the dilemma is to make him or her like me, no longer an alien. That is, of course, infinitely better than the opposite—exclusion, repression, and worse. But it is still a form of dangerous internal and external intolerance.

The alternative strategy of dealing with the alien is to acknowledge the validity of certain forms of (nonethnic) bounded identity but simultaneously to reach across boundaries. We acknowledge and respect difference, and yet we strive to go beyond our differences in recognition of our common humanity. On the one hand, the identity of the alien, as such, is maintained. We are not invited to go out and, say, "save" a person by inviting him or her to become one of us. On the other hand, despite the boundaries that are maintained, we are commanded to reach over the boundary and accept his or her alienship as we accept ourselves. In other words, the alien is accorded human dignity. The soul of the "I" is tended to not by eliminating the temptation to oppress but by learning humility and overcoming it.

The current European constitutional architecture represents this alternative civilizing strategy of dealing with the "other." Constitutional tolerance is encapsulated in that most basic articulation of its metapolitical objective, again the preamble to the original treaty establishing the European Community: "Determined to lay the foundations of an ever closer union among the peoples of Europe." No matter how close the union, it is to remain a union of distinct peoples, distinct political identities, and distinct political communities. An ever closer union could be achieved by an amalgam of distinct peoples into one, which is both the ideal or the de facto experience, or both, of most federal and nonfederal states. Europe's rejection of the "one nation" ideal is, as indicated above, usually understood as intended to preserve the rich diversity—cultural and other—of the distinct European peoples as well as to respect their political self-determination. But the European choice has an even deeper spiritual meaning.

An ever closer union is altogether easier to achieve if differences among the components are eliminated, if they come to resemble each other, if they aspire to become one. It is altogether more difficult to attain an ever closer union if the components of that union preserve their distinct identities, if they retain their "otherness" vis-à-vis each other, if they do not, politically speaking, become "one flesh." Herein resides the *principle of tolerance*. Inevitably, I define my distinct identity by a boundary that differentiates me from those who are unlike me. My continued existence as a distinct identity depends, ontologically, on that boundary and, psychologically and sociologically, on preserving that sentiment of otherness. The call to bond with those very others in an ever closer union demands internalization—individual and societal—of a very high degree of tolerance. Living the Kantian categorical imperative is most meaningful when it is extended to those who are unlike me.

In political terms, the principle of tolerance finds a remarkable expression in the political organization of the European Union, which defies the normal premise of formal constitutionalism. Normally in a democracy, we demand democratic discipline—that is, acceptance of the authority of the majority over the minority—but only within a polity that understands itself as being constituted of one people, however defined. The demanding of obedience by a majority from a minority that does not regard itself as belonging to the same people is usually regarded as subjugation. That is even more so in relation to constitutional discipline. And yet, in the Community, we subject the European peoples to constitutional discipline even though the European polity is composed of distinct peoples situated within distinct constitutional orders. It is a remarkable instance of civic tolerance to accept to be bound by precepts articulated not by "my people" but by a community composed of distinct political communities—a people, if you wish, of others. Constitutionally, the principle of tolerance finds its expression in the very arrangement that has now come under discussion: a federal constitutional discipline that is not rooted in a statal type of formal constitution.

Constitutional actors in the member states accept the European constitutional discipline as an autonomous, voluntary act of subordination. Of course, to do so creates in itself a different type of political community, one unique feature of which is that very willingness to accept a binding discipline that is rooted in and derives from a community of others. The Quebecois are told, "In the name of the People of Canada, you are obliged to obey." The French or the Italians or the Germans are told, "In the name of the peoples of Europe, you are invited to obey." In both, constitutional obedience is demanded. When acceptance and subordination is voluntary, and repeatedly so, it constitutes an act of true liberty and emancipation—a high expression of constitutional tolerance.

The principle of constitutional tolerance is not a one-way concept—it applies to constitutional actors and constitutional transactions at the member-state level, at the Union level, and among the member states too. Constitutional tolerance is, in my view, most present in the sphere of public administration, in the habits and practices that it instills in the purveyors of public power in European states, from the most mundane to the most august. At the most mundane administrative level, imagine immigration officials examining the passports of Union nationals in the same line and with the same scrutiny as they examine those of their own nationals, thereby overturning decades- and centuries-old practices.

Likewise, a similar discipline will become routine in policymaking forums. In a myriad of areas, whether a local council or a parliament itself, every norm, every policy will be subject to an unofficial European impact study. Many of them will no longer be able to be adopted without examining their consonance with the interest of others, the interest of Europe. Think, too, of the judicial function, ranging from the neighborhood *giudice conciliatore* to the highest jurisdictions: European law, the interest of others, is part of the judicial normative matrix.

I have deliberately chosen examples that are both daily and commonplace but that also overturn what until recently would have been considered important constitutional distinctions. This process also operates at the Union level. Think of the European judge or the European public official who must understand that in the peculiar constitutional compact of Europe, his or her decision will take effect only if obeyed by judges on the national courts and executed faithfully by national public officials, both of whom belong to a national administration that claims from them an especially strong form of loyalty and habit. That, too, will instill a measure of caution and tolerance.

What defines the European constitutional architecture is not the exception. It is the quotidian, the daily practices, even if done unthinkingly, even if executed in such a way because the new staff regulations require it. That praxis habituates its practitioners at all levels of public administration to these concealed virtues.

To extol the extant constitutional arrangement of Europe is not to suggest that many of its specifics cannot be vastly improved. The Treaty can be pared down considerably, competences can be better protected,[14] and vast changes can be introduced to its institutional arrangements. But to the critics who object that there is nothing to prevent a European constitution from being drafted in a way that would fully recognize the very concepts and principles that I have articulated, my answer is simple: Europe has now such a constitution. Europe has charted its own brand of constitutional federalism.

CONCLUSIONS:
THE ACCIDENTAL CONSTITUTION AND EUROPE 2030

It was and still is common to compare Europe to a bicycle: if it stops moving, it falls.[15] That notion has become pervasive in the political culture and in practice—one intergovernmental conference chasing another in a never-ending effort to achieve progress. The Constitution submitted to the European peoples in 2004—and rejected by them—was just part of that pattern. It was begotten by political hubris rather than constitutional necessity. Thus, in a public speech not long before the Treaty establishing a Constitution for Europe "bit the dust," Valéry Giscard d'Estaing opined: "The word 'constitution' implies not only a legal system, but more than that. . . . One single text would create the legal existence of Europe."[16] In that commonly held view, Europe was *sans constitution* until the 2004 project was presented to the European peoples—and rejected. I have presented in this essay the alternative thesis, far from radical in legal circles, that although it is based on international treaties, the European system, bit by bit, without a grand design—accidentally—evolved into an original and unique constitutional framework. From a constitutional point of view, that framework not only has served it well but also has been remarkably stable. Normatively, to suggest that the current, patchy, treaty-based framework is "Europe's constitutional promised land," accidently stumbled upon, may be thought of as an idiosyncratic view of a conservative lawyer privileging the status quo. Moreover, to predict that the constitutional terrain twenty years from now will be essentially the same as it is today will no doubt be thought of as a lack of political and legal imagination and creativity. Perhaps it is.

But imagine that fifty years after the adoption of the U.S. Constitution the same question was put to an American observer and the observer predicted that—fifty years hence, one hundred years hence, one hundred fifty years hence—the basic constitutional framework would still be the same. To be sure, the United States went through its Civil War and there have been a number of notable constitutional moments, but, essentially, that prediction would have proven correct. The stability of the U.S. Constitution is one of its great virtues.

It was predicted that Europe would implode without the reforms that were part of the "constitutional" design. But it continued to roll on happily, and the Lisbon Treaty will grease the wheels further. The very resilience and stability of the present constitutional framework is testimony to its soundness.

The rejection of the Constitution will prove to be a very positive event if Europe learns its lesson and does not repeat the error of hubris and obsession with progress at the root of its recent constitutional debacle. If Europe is able to leave one of its singular achievements, a constitutional framework that is both noble and functional, alone, then in its essentials, Europe 2030 will be—and should be—constitutionally the same as Europe 2010 and Europe 2050. A wise European, Seneca, summed it up well: *Errarum humanum est, perseverare diabolicum.*

NOTES

1. Joschka Fischer set the ball rolling. For text and discussion, see Cristian Joerges, Yves Mény, and Joseph H. H. Weiler, eds., "What Kind of Constitution for What Kind of Polity? Responses to Joschka Fischer" (Florence, Italy: Robert Schuman Centre, European University Institute/Harvard Law School, 2000). See too the op-ed piece by Valéry Giscard d'Estaing and Helmut Schmidt, *International Herald Tribune*, April 11, 2000.

2. Jürgen Habermas, "So, Why Does Europe Need a Constitution?" originally published as "Warum braucht Europa eine Verfassung?" in *Zeit der Übergänge* (2001), pp. 104–29. Jürgen Habermas, "Citoyenneté et identité nationale. Réflexions sur l'avenir de l'Europe," in *L'Europe au Soir du Siècle: Identité et Démocratie*, edited by Jacques Lenoble and Nicole Dewandre (Paris: Esprit, 1992); Jürgen Habermas, "The European Nation-State and the Pressures of Globalization," *New Left Review* 235 (1999), pp. 46–59; Joseph H. H. Weiler, "Does Europe Need a Constitution? Demos, Telos, and the German Maastricht Decision," *European Law Journal* 1 (1995), p. 219.

3. Compare Joseph H. H. Weiler, "Federalism without Constitutionalism: Europe's Sonderweg," in *The Federal Vision: Legitimacy and Levels of Governance in the United States and the European Union*, edited by Kalypso Nicolaïdis and Robert Howse (Oxford University Press, 2001).

4. Daniel J. Elazar, *Self-Rule/Shared Rule: Federal Solutions to the Middle East Conflict* (Israel: Turtledove Publishers, 1979). p. 3.

5. Pierre Pescatore, Preface, "Courts and Free Markets," in *Courts and Free Markets*, vol. 1, edited by Terrance Sandalow and Eric Stein (Oxford University Press, 1982), pp. ix–x.

6. See, for example, Robert R. Bowie and Carl J. Friedrich, *Studies in Federalism* (Boston: Little Brown and Company, 1954) and Arthur Whittier Macmahon, *Federalism, Mature and Emergent* (New York: Doubleday and Company, 1955) for early comparative analysis in the formative years of European federalism. For subsequent analyses of the more mature system see, for example, Terrance Sandalow and Eric Stein, *Courts and Free Markets*; Mauro Cappelletti, Monica Seccombe, and Joseph H. H. Weiler, *Integration through Law: Europe and the American Federal Experience* (Berlin and New York: Walter de Gruyter, 1985); Koen Lenaerts, *Two Hundred Years of U.S. Constitution and Thirty Years of EEC Treaty* (Brussels: Kluwer, 1988).

7. Originally Article 189 EEC (Treaty of Rome).

8. The general rule of international law does not allow, except in the narrowest of circumstances, for a state to use its own domestic law, including its own domestic constitutional law, as an excuse for nonperformance of a treaty. That is part of the ABCs of international law and is reflected in the same Vienna Convention Article 27. Oppenheim's International Law is clear: "It is firmly established that a state when charged with a breach of its international obligations cannot in international law validly plead as a defense that it was unable to fulfill them because its internal law . . . contained rules in conflict with international law; this applies equally to a state's assertion of its inability to secure the necessary changes in its law by virtue of some legal or constitutional requirement." Sir Robert Jennings and Sir Arthur Watts, *Oppenheim's International Law*, vol. 1, 9th ed., *Peace* (Harlow, Essex: Longmans, 1992), pp. 84–85.

9. See generally Joseph H. H. Weiler, "The Transformation of Europe," in *The Constitution of Europe* (Cambridge University Press, 1999).

10. See three classics: Alan S. Milward and others, *The European Rescue of the Nation State* (University of California Press, 1993); Stanley Hoffmann, "Reflections on the Nation-State in Western Europe Today," in *The European Community: Past, Present, and Future*, edited by Loukas Tsoukalis (Oxford: Basil Blackwell, 1983); and Andrew Moravcsik, *The Choice for Europe* (Cornell University Press, 1998).

11. See, for example, the op-ed by Valéry Giscard d'Estaing and Helmut Schmidt in note 1 *supra*. For a more honest discussion admitting the statal implications of the new construct, see, for example, G. Federico Mancini, "Europe: The Case for State-hood," *European Law Journal* 4, no.1 (March 1998), pp. 29–42, and, of course, Habermas. There is an interesting political-legal paradox here. A "flexible" Europe with a "core" at its center will actually enable that core to retain the present governance system, dominated by the Council—the executive branch of the member states—at the expense of national parliamentary democracy. Constitutionally, the statal structure would in fact enhance the democracy deficit even further.

12. Koen Lenaerts, "Constitutionalism and the Many Faces of Federalism," *American Journal of Comparative Law* 38 (1990), pp. 205–63 at 220. The Court, too, has modified its rhetoric: In its more recent Opinion 1/91 it refers to the member states as having limited their sovereign rights "in ever wider fields." Opinion 1/91 [1991], ECR 6079, Recital 21.

13. Miguel Poiares Maduro, *We, The Court: The European Court of Justice and the European Economic Constitution* (Oxford: Hart Publishing, 1998), p. 175. Maduro himself does not advocate a European constitution. I cite him simply for his striking diagnosis of the issue. It is superior to my own clumsy attempt to formulate the dilemma as a "Constitution without Constitutionalism," as "doing before hearkening." Joseph H. H. Weiler, "We Will Do, and Hearken' (Ex. XXIV: 7): Reflections on a Common Constitutional Law for the European Union," in *The European Constitutional Area*, edited by Roland Bieber and Pierre Widmer (Zurich: Schulthess, 1995), p. 413.

14. The issue of competences is especially acute since there has been a considerable weakening of constitutional guarantees to the limits of Community competences, undermining constitutional tolerance itself. See Bruno Simma, Joseph H. H. Weiler, and Markus C. Zöckler, *Kompetenzen und Grundrechte—Beschränkungen der Tabakwerbung aus der Sicht des Europarechts* (Berlin: Duncker & Humblot, 1999). History teaches that formal constitutions tend to strengthen the center, whatever the good intentions of their authors. Any formulation designed to restore constitutional discipline on this issue can be part of a Treaty revision and would not require a constitution. For pragmatic proposals on this issue, see J. H. H. Weiler and others, *Certain Rectangular Problems of European Integration* (1996) (www.europarl.europa.eu/activities/committees/studies.do).

15. For a mammoth collection of the use of the metaphor, see Andreas Musolff, "Bicycle Metaphors in Euro-Debates in Britain and Germany [Fahrradmetaphern in Europadebatten]" (www.dur.ac.uk/andreas.musolff/bicycle.pdf).

16. Second Annual Emile Noel Lecture, 2005, New York University School of Law (www.jeanmonetprogram.org).

ANDREW HILTON

4

The European Economic Model in 2030

It all depends on what you mean by "European" . . .

EVEN BEFORE THE future of capitalism itself was put in question by the crisis that broke with the collapse of the U.S. subprime mortgage market, a real battle of ideas was taking place over the concept of "Europe"—a battle that colors everything that the European nation-states do and one that the United States doesn't begin to understand.

The reason that many Americans do not understand it is that this battle does not accord with what most U.S. euro-watchers fondly believe to be their own history. Of course, if one looks back to the U.S. founding fathers, one sees that Washington, Hamilton, and the like had an economic vision of the newly independent colonies that is not too far removed from the vision that empowered EFTA (the European Free Trade Area) or the EEA (the European Economic Area) but that is a good deal further removed from the vision of the EU's founding fathers (Schuman, de Gasperi, and so forth). After all, what the early Americans were most interested in was free trade and the free movement of people and goods; initially at least, taxation was an issue to be left to individual states. In contrast, the European Union's founding fathers were obsessed from the outset with melding the Continental European economies together, in large part so that Germany would never again have sole control over enough industrial resources to pose a military threat to its neighbors.

The fact that the American founding fathers' vision broke down quite quickly into the simpler idea of a unitary state—particularly after the defeat of the confederal view, as a result of the Civil War—should not obscure the original, more limited, less centralized, vision of the New America that prevailed after the British were kicked out. Unfortunately, however, it often does. Today, the view of Europe from Washington stems from the views of policymakers, many of whom are first- or second-generation European immigrants, whose understanding of European politics is a legacy of the bad old days of *mitteleuropean* nationalism. It is quite natural that they saw and see a unitary European state, with all the economic and fiscal trimmings, as a consummation devoutly to be wished. Equally, it is quite natural that they see the doubts of those like Václav Klaus, Donald Tusk, and the British euroskeptics as recidivist, perverse, and somehow against the tide of history.

Maybe they're right. But what they forget—or never really knew—is the early history of their own country and how it might well have taken a very different course if the surprisingly limited ambitions of the founding fathers and subsequent generations had not been overwhelmed by a wave of European immigrants who brought with them a very different conception of what government is supposed to do.

In other words, one should not fall into the easy assumption that Europe—be it a Europe of six, nine, fifteen, twenty-seven, or more members—is heading ineluctably toward a single state or a simple economic union on the U.S. model. And don't slag off those who oppose that tendency as ahistorical, chauvinistic, or just plain thick. Even in the present economic and financial morass, the economic and political underpinnings of the federalist movement in Europe are dodgy, at best.

So, where does that leave us?

Over the next few decades, assuming that the EU overcomes the immediate crisis, there is going to be a fight for the soul of Europe—or more accurately, albeit more prosaically, over the political and economic direction that the EU should take. At this point, it is utterly unclear what faction will prevail, and it is quite possible in any case that the decisive elements will come from outside—that is, that the shape of "Europe" will be determined not in Brussels, Paris, or London but in Moscow, Beijing, or, though less likely, Washington. That possibility is especially apparent in the economic sphere, since, for the moment at least, the EU as a whole is far more open and far more integrated into the global economy than is the relatively autarchic United States.

Maybe the economic and political centralizers—known in Europe, perversely, as "federalists"—will win. Maybe all or a significant subset of the twenty-seven current EU members will be, twenty years from now, a single unitary state, with a single unitary government, a genuine single market, and all the usual appurtenances thereto. And maybe pigs will fly. I would put the following proposition on the table: It is more likely that the political unity of the United States will be in jeopardy twenty years from now than that there will be a true "United States of Europe."

Of course, that does not mean that twenty years from now the EU will be defunct or that it will be even more fragmented than it is today. It is simply to say that the political and economic future of Europe is essentially unknowable, and it would be foolish to assert with any confidence that the EU is on a particular track to a particular political destination. Instead, there is a range of possible outcomes, to which one might attach probabilities—though those probabilities will probably reveal less about the world than about the prejudices of those assigning them. Left to right across your radio dial, they include:

—a genuine United States of Europe, including EU applicant states, the EEA and Switzerland, and conceivably Turkey, Russia, and Israel

—an ersatz United States of Europe, comprising more or less the original six members of the European Economic Community (EEC-6), plus a few small, enthusiastic states, like Slovenia and Ireland

—a two-tier EU, in which a core of enthusiastic centralizers presses ahead with something more or less like a real state, while the rest of the twenty-seven (or more) sign up only for country club membership

—a "variable geometry" EU, in which all members are required to sign up to a fairly minimal *acquis communautaire*, after which they can pick and choose—"one from column A and two from column B" (for those old enough to remember the *Firesign Theater*)

—a much looser arrangement based on the free movement of goods, services, and labor—possibly with some restrictions on the last—and not much else.

Of course, there is also the possibility of a simple continuation of the status quo, in which the European project lurches from crisis to crisis, with elites perpetually bewildered why *hoi polloi* do not share their enthusiasm for something that is so obviously good for them. Naturally, the most fervent "Europeans" see the current economic crisis as vindication of a "European" economic model and as a repudiation of the "Anglo-Saxon" way of organizing things. They therefore hope that, in some way, the outcome of the crisis will be a widening of the Atlantic and a closer bonding of, at least, the Continental EU member states.

Maybe. But it is also worth bearing in mind the condemnation by former German finance minister Steinbrück of Italian prime minister Berlusconi's idea for a common EU bailout fund. Germany, Steinbrück said, would *never* join a bailout fund over which it did not have control. No bailing out the spendthrift southern Europeans, thank you—which is not a very *communautaire* approach.

The point is that *any discussion of what shape the EU's economic model will take over the next twenty years depends overwhelmingly on the direction that Europe itself will take.* If the EU does move to a single political entity, it is a safe bet that there will be a genuine single market within the EU, in which broadly the same rules apply in all states, with a common currency, harmonized corporate taxation, a single central bank (though national central banks may continue to act as agents), and a single financial regulator. There will also be harmonization of consumer protection rules, health and safety legislation, clearing and settlement systems, *und so weiter*. However, if Europe does not move in that direction—and I am doubtful that it will—then the situation becomes much more complicated. That is not to say that there will not be some sort of evolution to a common "European" economic model—or, in my own particular field of expertise, a single financial regulator. There may well be, but neither proposition is a shoo-in.

First, let's look at where the EU is today. There is no single "European" economic model—however much euro-enthusiasts might like to pretend that there is. What exists is a union of more or less independent nation-states, derived from the postwar European Coal and Steel Community, that has entered into a series of treaties designed to create a single market in goods and services and a single trade and tariff policy vis-à-vis the external world.

Even a euroskeptic would have to accept that a great deal of progress has been made with regard to integration—more so in the economic sphere than in the political. Thanks to the treaties of Rome, Maastricht, and Nice, the EU genuinely does have free movement of goods and services among its members (of course, thanks to the WTO, it also has fairly free movement of goods and services from outside the EU); it also has free movement of people, though not *all* people. Several member states, for instance, have retained the right to exclude nationals of the newer EU member states, at least temporarily.

There is also a single currency area, the eurozone—though it currently excludes the United Kingdom, the Scandinavian countries, and most of the former Soviet satellites. With the single currency comes a single central bank, the European Central Bank (ECB), which sets reference interest rates for the bloc as a whole—though, it should be noted, so far that has not meant any significant job losses at the national central bank (NCB) level. Assuming the Treaty of Nice is ratified, it will also have an independent legal identity and a fledgling foreign service—but not much more.

To date, the euro and the ECB have been real successes. Even a euroskeptic must acknowledge that the ECB looks a lot more like the old Bundesbank, with its monomaniacal focus on inflation, than, say, the Bank of Greece. But it is worth emphasizing that it has not yet come under real pressure. As the economic conjuncture deteriorates, political pressures on the bank will build up, and it will be sorely tested—and it might well be unable to resist if, say, France and Germany decide to lean on it.

It is also worth looking at the credit markets' view of the eurozone. As the financial crisis escalated, interest rate spreads on ten-year government bonds within the eurozone rose from 10 to 15 basis points to 125 or more. Plus, credit default swap rates on eurozone sovereigns increased sharply. The markets were clearly trying to tell us something. Things are looking better now (in late 2009)—but it isn't just a few crazy academics who expect 2010 to be a *very* difficult year.

But is there a single economic model—even a single economic philosophy—behind all of this? The answer is clearly no. At the risk of gross oversimplification, let me suggest that there are several European economic models—many of which are overlapping, competing, more or less incompatible, and often quite useless.

At one end of the ideological spectrum—the currently unfashionable end—is a sort of milquetoast version of American capitalism. This version was traditionally embraced with greater or lesser enthusiasm by the United Kingdom, Ireland, the Baltic States, Poland, and perhaps the Netherlands—though Ireland and the Balts may be having second thoughts. It looks a bit like the United States, but with the sharp corners smoothed off. We talk loosely of Thatcherism—and, indeed, the U.K. economy underwent a magical transformation, as did its political clout, under her premiership. But Americans should remember that Thatcher's name is now reviled, not only among the euro-elites but even in her own country and, incidentally, by the new leaders of her own party.

Under Tony Blair and Gordon Brown, and even under John Major before them, the United Kingdom began peddling furiously in the opposite direction, away from its Thatcherite legacy—ditching the red-in-tooth-and-claw free market model that is now pretty much taken for granted in the United States. As a result, the United Kingdom has moved, according to the OECD's classification, from a low- to a medium-tax economy; indeed, the total tax burden is now heavier in Britain than it is in Germany, and it will get even heavier. Nevertheless, since perceptions tend to lag reality, the UK is still *perceived* to be at the "robust" end of the spectrum and is excoriated as a result by those who believe that one man's prosperity can be built only on the immiseration of others—a common view in some Continental European countries.

With respect to the other end of the spectrum, well, there is not actually a single other end. Rather, there are several different economic models, often coexisting uneasily within the same country, all tending to define themselves more or less vehemently in contradistinction to the Anglo-Saxon, Thatcherite model that is, again, widely—though inaccurately—believed still to prevail across the English Channel.

First, there are the Scandinavians—widely pilloried as well-meaning, earnest, eco-friendly exponents of a high-tax, welfare-based system, in which the egalitarian impulse is said to outpunch fear and greed. The result is lower growth than in the Anglo-Saxon countries but a less offensive income distribution. It is still broadly a private sector model—but just. There is some truth in that caricature. But the exigencies of economic reality do creep in, and as economic growth rates have fallen, many of the Scandinavian countries have moved a bit to the right.

Moving sharply to the left is France—if by "left" one means support of economic nationalism and protectionism such as used to be espoused by the Poujadist right. Nowadays, notwithstanding Sarkozy's initial enthusiasm for the United States, France is in the vanguard of eurochavismo—talking, once again, of "national champions," undermining the WTO, and threatening retaliation against allegedly low-tax competitors in or outside the EU. That is a perennial French foible that never seems to lose its luster.

Germany under the popular Angela Merkel is a swing vote. However, the fastest-growing party in Germany today is Oskar Lafontaine's (unreconstructed) left—which is closer to the ex–Communist Party of Democratic Socialism than it is to the two mainstream parties. Spain is also under pressure to move to the left, thanks to a politically devastating commercial property bust, as are Poland and Greece (which has, indeed, just elected a new Socialist government).

The result is that, on the key parameters of capitalism—levels of personal and corporate taxation, government's role in the economy, openness to trade and investment, and so forth—Europe is a mish-mash. The current crisis has only reinforced that description as EU member states talk of joint action and then reject it when the threat of bailing out the feckless rears its head. European politicians and bureaucrats may pretend otherwise, but anyone who travels throughout the EU, not just in the eurozone, must be more impressed with the divergence of economic approaches and structures than with their sameness. Nowhere is the gap between perception and reality more obvious than in the financial services sector—which, because it encapsulates the problems that the eurofederalists face, is worth a closer look.

Financial services were one of the main economic activities slated for a common EU-wide approach as early as 1985, with the release of the Cockfield Report. But progress toward harmonization of the rules for the cross-border provisioning of financial services has been painful and slow, prompting the FSAP (Financial Services Action Plan) in 1998. The FSAP was a wish-list of forty-two measures that the European Commission of the time believed were necessary to make a single market in financial services throughout the EU a reality. Most but not quite all of those measures have been rammed through Brussels, either as directives or regulations, but very few people would say that there is, at this time, a true single market in financial services. And, with the commission's priorities somewhat distracted, a true single market does not seem to be on the horizon.

Why not? Well, the first thing to understand is that the concept of a single market in financial services in the EU is much less meaningful than euro-enthusiasts would have one believe. For example, consider the following:

—Do I really want to open a checking account in, say, Greece or Romania? Answer: No, not any more than someone who lives in Carroll Gardens, Brooklyn, would want to open a checking account with the Third Bank of Podunk.

—Do I really want a mortgage from a Bulgarian or Finnish bank? Answer: Well, I might—if the interest rate was a lot lower or the terms a lot less arduous. But housing finance is pretty idiosyncratic, and what counts as a mortgage in one country is hardly recognizable as such in another.

—Do I want to buy life insurance or a pension or some other kind of long-term savings product from a Lithuanian or Hungarian institution? Answer: Well, again, one might—but it would have to have a pretty good offer to offset the problems of doing business in a different time zone, in a different language, and under a different legal system.

I am not saying that there has been no progress in the financial area. The Woolwich, for instance (now owned by Barclays), had some success selling U.K.-style variable rate mortgages in Holland and Belgium, and Greeks seem fairly happy buying longer-term savings products from French and German institutions, though *not vice versa*. There is also a modest, but genuine, cross-border market in mutual fund–type vehicles, with Luxembourg and Ireland in the vanguard. But, for the most part, there is not a huge consumer-driven demand for a single European market in financial services, even within the eurozone. It is an elite, or bureaucratic, conceit—and therefore has to be kept alive by frequent appeals to a *communautaire* spirit that is still, in most EU member states, sadly lacking. It is unlikely that the current crisis—which is forcing consolidation in both the retail and investment banking sectors—is really going to change that. Nor should it.

The point is that, for the most part, Europeans are fairly comfortable with the idea that they should buy financial services locally—where they understand the language, the idiosyncratic product offer, the legal underpinnings, and, not least, the remedies available if anything goes wrong. For better or worse, this is a lesson that applies to many other economic activities too. And, contrary to self-serving reports from the European Commission or the European Parliament, there is no real evidence that Europeans suffer appreciably as a result. Strange as it may seem, a strong case can be made that, in the financial services sector, the problem in Europe is *too much* competition, not too little.

The second point is that—just as there exists an Anglo-Saxon economic model and a variety of Continental alternatives—there also exist very different conceptions of financial services throughout Europe. In recent years, they have converged somewhat, and—following the Northern Rock debacle in the United Kingdom and the whole U.S. subprime mess—it is no longer so axiomatic that one model is better than any other. But key differences remain, and the models do not fit together easily:

—The first is the Anglo-Saxon/U.S.-U.K. model, with which an American readership is broadly familiar. It treats financial services much like any other sector—albeit more heavily regulated than, say, the manufacture of widgets.

—The others include the several variants of the Continental model, which see financial services as essentially a utility, more like the provision of water or electricity than, say, retailing.

Of course, at times they do come together. Indeed, in a recent pamphlet for the CSFI (entitled "Narrow Banking"), John Kay, a prominent U.K. economist, describes the Western banking world as "a utility with a casino built on."

Within the EU, the United Kingdom and Ireland sit at one end of the spectrum. At the other end is Germany—and it is no coincidence that as the credit crisis was unwinding, senior German politicians were seriously proposing that the top four German banks (Deutsche Bank, Dresdner Bank, Commerz Bank, and Postbank) merge their retail operations into one utility-like behemoth. As Europe moves left, as I believe it will, more of this kind of romanticism will be heard. At the same time, there are the Scandinavians, Baltics, and Nordics, where there has been genuine cross-border consolidation, and Poland, where there is not a single nationally owned bank. There also is Spain, which looks increasingly to Latin America; Greece, which looks to the Balkans; and Slovakia, where gangsters rule.

The third thing to understand is the decisionmaking process within Europe—and that applies to all economic activities, not just financial services. However, since financial services are fundamental, they make a good poster child for any critique of EU decisionmaking.

It is widely and loudly said by Europeans that the U.S. financial regulatory system is so awful that no one in his or her right mind would ever try to replicate it—and former secretary of the treasury Paulson would appear to agree. But one should not fall into the trap of assuming that the EU system is a paragon of rationality. Far from it: it is the result of fierce bargaining between member states, community institutions, and key individuals—and some of the trade-offs had nothing to do with finance. The location of one level-3 financial regulatory committee, for instance, was settled only when the United Kingdom agreed to support France's bid to house the EU's nuclear research facility. Moreover, the EU's regulatory system is in a state of flux; by the time this chapter is in print, it may well have changed, given the new European Parliament, the new European Commission, and the fundamental review of the FSAP already under way.

How to summarize the current situation?

Well, first there's a thing called co-decision, or "comitology." That means that the three key EU institutions—the Council, made up of ministers from individual member states; the Parliament, made up of elected representatives, grouped into more-or-less-real pan-European parties; and the Commission, the career bureaucrats in Brussels, with the addition of superannuated national politicians "parachuted" in at the top—all have a say in making economic and financial policy. But not an equal say. The Commission, to many observers' surprise, has a monopoly on initiating legislation; the Parliament (which is on a long-term power grab), has an increasingly effective veto; the Council has to sign off formally on anything significant; and the Council president, currently on a six-month rotation through all twenty-seven members (though that will change now that the Irish were "convinced" to rescind their rejection of the European Constitution), gets to set the broad agenda for the union itself.

So, to take the example of financial services, the forty-two components of the FSAP were dreamed up by the Commission—or rather by a mysterious cabal called DG-Markt (Internal Market and Services Directorate General) and formerly known, even more cryptically, as DG-15. The 2009 commissioner of DG-Markt, Charlie McCreevy, was an amiable, if completely incomprehensible, Irishman with a fondness for the horses that often took him away from Brussels. Generally, he was liked in London, which wants Brussels to do as little as possible in the financial services area, and held in contempt almost everywhere else in Europe. He is not seeking reappointment—and wouldn't get it if he were since no one except the British and Irish give him even a passing grade as commissioner.

DG-Markt doesn't always get its own way. Indeed, the Parliament has a committee that deals with finance (confusingly called ECON) and that sticks its oar in at every opportunity. Its former chairwoman, Pervenche Berès (the Barney Frank of Brussels, if you will) was an unreconstructed French socialist of the Rosa Luxemburg variety; she and pinstripe bankers were not a natural fit. Fortunately, she is being replaced by a British patent lawyer—but she, too, is no friend to finance.

And then, of course, there's ECOFIN—the monthly meeting of the EU-27 economic and finance ministers and their deputies that has to put its John Hancock on any new directive, albeit by qualified majority vote (QMV). QMV is important and not just in the financial area. Effectively, it means that the United Kingdom (America's friend at the euro-court) can be outvoted by a minicoalition of microstates—Lithuania, Luxembourg, Slovenia, and Slovakia, say.

In other words, it's a nightmare. For years, the Brits clung to control of what was then DG-15—realizing that financial services are to the United Kingdom what olive oil is to Italy, wine to France, or gas-guzzling automobiles are to Germany. But even that small part of a foreign field is no longer England; it is now firmly continentalized. And DG-Comp (formerly DG-24), which handles competition matters and is utterly statist, is also starting to get its paws on economic affairs and financial services—with a distinctly uncapitalist agenda.

This approach is replicated across the full range of economic activities. In each, there is a continuing battle between the idiosyncratic structures and preferences of the nation-states and the powers-that-be in Brussels. The eurocrats are keen centralizers; they are also astute politicians—even (perhaps especially) those who have nothing to do with formal party politics. Their aim is the steady accretion of power—and the progressive drawing away of influence from national authorities.

They are good at that. But it is important to understand that it is not a process that has any democratic legitimacy or popular mandate. Indeed, even in the most *communautaire* of EU member states, wherever there is a vote on the transfer of power to Brussels, it tends to get rejected. (Ireland is not really a counterexample, given the enormous pressure that had to be applied to such a tiny country to get it to "vote right.") But that's not the half of it.

Recognizing that the regulation of financial services is important and that regulations need to change to reflect changing realities, Brussels some years ago adopted a scheme dreamed up by a Belgian-Hungarian baron, Alexandre Lamfalussy. The Lamfalussy process created a three-level hierarchy of committees, culminating in a trinity of euro-rulemakers—CEBS, CESR and CEIOPS, the so-called level-3 committees. CEBS (Committee of European Banking Supervisors) is in London; CESR (Committee of European Securities Regulators) is in Paris; CEIOPS (Committee of European Insurance and Occupational Pensions Supervisors) is, for no good reason, in Madrid.

Perhaps I should also explain that all this pan-EU palaver coexists uneasily with twenty-seven national regulatory structures—including the biggest of the bunch, the U.K. Financial Services Authority, which now has close to 2,000 employees and is, in effect, the international supervisor of choice for many of the biggest financial services firms in the world. It also has to coexist with global and regional organizations—like the Basel Committee at the BIS (Bank for International Settlements) and IOSCO (International Organization of Securities Commissions)—that, while they have no direct rulemaking authority, expect their decisions to be quickly translated into national legislation.

I could also try to summarize the home–host issue; the curious role of the European Central Bank, whose mandate specifically excludes supervision yet which has a substantial stability department; the treatment of branches and subsidiaries; and the problem of insurance or that of deposit guarantee schemes. But the point is that in financial services, as in any economic area, there are competing interests, competing institutions, and competing pressures between national and "European" politicians—none of which seems likely to be successfully addressed any time soon, particularly not at this economic "conjuncture." My favorite mathematical factoid is that if there are ten variables that determine the future, there are factorial 10 futures—or just slightly under 1 million. In this case, there are considerably more than ten factors that will determine what the EU's economic model will look like twenty years from now. *So, let's stop trying to guess.* Let's put on the table instead what key interest groups appear to want—or *vice versa*—and what kind of futures are endorsed by what sorts of interest groups.

First, there are the true believers, the good Europeans, the arch-federalists, who believe that, in the end, if there is to be a "European" economy, then there must be a centralization of power in Brussels, a clear shift of economic power from nation-states to the center—and, ultimately, a realization by the so-called Anglo-Saxons that their model will have to give way to some variant of the "softer" Continental approach. I wouldn't rule it out altogether—particularly if the economic crisis deepens. As I said, there is a tide in Europe that is running against the U.S. ship of state and all who sail in her—as evidenced by repeated Pew surveys. For the moment, the high-growth/low-tax model is in retreat, in favor of an allegedly "softer, kinder" economic philosophy. But these things are cyclical, and twenty years is a very long time ahead.

For the moment, however, that's the direction the EU is moving in—and it is very noticeable in the financial services sector in the call for a single financial regulator. Because the Anglo-Saxon model is followed in only a minority of EU member states, it is argued that the regulator should not be the UK's Financial Services Authority (FSA), with its allegedly discredited principles-based approach. Logically, in the federalists' view, it probably should be an adjunct of the ECB in Frankfurt, though there are ultra-romantics who argue that CESR (the Lamfalussy committee that brings together EU securities regulators)—which just happens to be based in Paris—could transmogrify into a pan-European financial services regulator.

It is hard to find anyone who knows anything about financial services who subscribes to this vision publicly—though I have heard very senior European parliamentarians get close. It is, however, safe to assume that most of the Continental socialists subscribe privately to it—and not a few Christian Democrats, as the center-right parties style themselves—and the perceived "failure" of the Anglo-Saxon model gives them an opportunity.

What they want is for the regulation and supervision of commercial and investment banking, insurance, fund management, private equity, hedge funds, and the rating agencies to be centralized, presumably under the wing of the ECB—which would also have responsibility for ensuring systemic stability and for overseeing the payment and settlement system (into which area it is moving forcefully, with its utterly unloved T2S payments/settlement project).

I have already indicated that I think that this is fanciful. Aside from the fact that no one really wants to live in Frankfurt, it would require national regulators (including the FSA behemoth) to become nothing more than ECB agencies, doing what they are told and nothing more.

Second, at the other end of the financial services scale are those (mostly in London, it has to be said) who get down on their knees each night to pray that the EU hits a rock, sinks, and is reborn as nothing more than a free trade area. For them, the ideal is that financial regulation is retained as a national competence, that individual regulators are bound only by the top-down harmonization of international bodies like Basel and IOSCO, and that the whole panoply of EU agencies and committees—not to mention the ECB itself—withers away. There would be no harmonization of deposit guarantee schemes, no attempt to force unnaturally the cross-border sale of financial products, no attempt to squeeze market-based, principles-based, Anglo-Saxon–style supervision into a narrowly prescriptive Napoleonic model that would, in their view, kill innovation, decimate the derivatives market, and drive business to Dubai, Qatar, Shanghai, Singapore—even back to New York.

Well, that won't happen either—particularly not in the present climate. So, all we euroskeptics—or eurorealists, as we like to be called—can weep into our beards. That is not to say, incidentally, that we don't have a point. In mid-2007, before the present crisis really boiled over, DG-Markt was floating an idea that would almost certainly drive a very large part of the securitization market out of London—should it ever recover, of course. The proposal, which is still being pursued with great vigor, is that EU investors would not be permitted to buy securitized paper unless either the originator or distributor of that paper committed to keep 10 or 20 percent on its own books. The laudable goal is to ensure that Goldman Sachs or Morgan Stanley or whoever is left has a continuing interest in the quality of the sausage meat that it grinds up and sells to final investors. The utterly predictable consequence will be to drive the business overseas—and, to those of a Continental persuasion, that would be no bad thing.

So, let's rule out both extremes. Let's also accept that exactly the same sort of battle is going on across the range of economic activities in

Europe—in telecoms, in pharmaceuticals, even in that bedrock of pan-European featherbedding, farming. Given how interests are balanced, it is hard to see either side winning a comprehensive victory; rather, the fight is over the middle ground, where both euro-enthusiasts and euroskeptics can feel cheated—the former because integration will not go as far as they feel that it should and the latter because any further integration will take place at all.

In my opinion—and I should add that this is a *descriptive* prediction, not a *normative* one—the following developments are more likely to happen than not in the financial services sector. It is a fair bet that they will be a proxy for developments in the economic space more broadly:

—Over time, the ECB will take on an increased role as a guarantor of systemic stability—initially within the eurozone but later within the wider EU. I accept that the eurozone itself may expand—but, frankly, the decision to admit Slovakia could just as easily blow it apart. And the widening of interest rate spreads between North and South suggests that, even without Slovakia, things could get a little hairy in the eurozone. The ECB wants this role, and few in Brussels will fight it.

—The enhancement of the ECB's powers will be accompanied, eventually, by formal recognition of the ECB as lender of last resort for the eurozone. At the moment, there is no such formal function within the eurozone, and the recent market turmoil has made it pretty clear that that is an oversight that needs to be corrected. With the ECB already going pell-mell into the payments and settlement area, this would be a natural expansion of its role.

—The three Lamfalussy committees, whose legal status is currently open to question, are already being formalized as "authorities" and will be given permanent staffs of their own. There are lots of problems with that, notably over what voting system they will adopt (at present, the best description is probably "qualified majority consensus"); however, it is a relatively safe bet that CEBS, CESR, and CEIOPS will continue in their new role, will grow in importance, and will have some sort of monitoring role, short of a veto, over national regulators.

—The increasing role of the European Parliament will bring it more and more into conflict with both the Commission and the Council—and financial services will be a particular testing ground since it will continue to be seen by Continental political lefties as stuffed full of fat cat capitalist pigs. Expect many, though fruitless, initiatives to restrict executive bonuses; cripple the rating agencies; hobble the last remaining U.S. investment banks, hedge funds, and private equity groups; and reverse the fragmentation of financial markets that was encouraged by the recent Markets in Financial Instruments Directive.

—Within the Commission, the British (Anglo-Saxon) hold over DG-Markt will continue to wither—in part because other governments will continue to pry British fingers off the key posts and in part because the U.K. government of the day will continue to fail to appreciate just how important DG-Markt is to the continued health of the City of London. As a result, my guess is that London will see continued erosion of its position in financial services in favor of centers like Dubai and Shanghai, though I accept that the knock-on effect of the current unpleasantness could see both Dubai and Shanghai in deep, deep trouble of their own. Linked to that, other DGs will increasingly interfere in the financial services area. Competition is already there, but there are some two dozen others—including Consumer Affairs, Health and Safety, Education, and Legal Services, among others. All of them have an angle that could impinge on the financial services sector.

What does this mean at a broader economic level?

First and foremost, it means that the Anglo-Saxon model (insofar as it is a model) will remain under pressure. However, it is worth making the point that Europe is not an actor with much autonomy in the global marketplace. Even if it overcomes the present crisis, even if we are not all back living in caves by 2030, there are lots of external forces that will constrain Europe's freedom of action. If, for instance, China continues to pump out goods that Europeans want at prices that they can afford and if European industry has to compete in the global marketplace with low-wage Asian producers, just how much authority will the center-left consensus in Continental Europe continue to exercise? Will there be a backlash? And if so, what form will it take? Will Europe ditch the Scandinavian social welfare model or the French model of national or European champions? Or will Europe, instead, opt out of the global trading system, dump the WTO, and retreat behind protectionist walls?

There is no doubt that opting out is a possibility. Indeed, it is the logical extension of the current rhetoric coming from Sarkozy, Berlusconi, et al. But it is worth remembering that, even at the worst of times, *consumers outnumber the unemployed*—even in Europe.

None of this is exactly earth-shattering. My personal view is that it is hard to overestimate the ability of a bureaucracy to muddle through—and muddling through is the most likely development over the next twenty years. But it is not a healthy environment for the U.S.-U.K. economic model or, indeed, for the European economy in the broader sense. The context in which economic actors will fight for their future over the next few years is one in which the dominant political sense in Europe is increasingly hostile to free-wheeling finance and is increasingly reluctant to risk another Bear Stearns or Lehman Brothers—or even another IKB Deutsche Industriebank or Société Générale.

5

Europe as a Global Actor in 2030

IN 2030 the European Union covers most of the European continent: it stretches from Iceland in the northwest to Ukraine in the east to Turkey in the southeast. It is one of the world's principal economic powers, and the euro matches the dollar and the yuan as a reserve currency. Politically, the EU is the dominant power in regions that are close to it, but further afield it is just one of a number of powers that matter. In that, it resembles China.

The EU can deploy up to 250,000 soldiers, given a few months' notice; they are usually sent on peacekeeping missions but occasionally are involved in combat. The EU also is the world's biggest provider of development aid. It is a champion of multilateral global governance, particularly on the issue of climate change. The International Carbon Fund, which regulates the world carbon market, is based in Strasbourg (it took over the buildings vacated by the European Parliament when that body moved to Brussels).

The EU has close ties with most of its neighbors, some of which take part in certain EU policies. The most problematic neighbor is Russia. Economically too weak to be a serious threat to the EU, Russia—known as the "sick man of Europe"—is large enough and prickly enough to be a frequent source of aggravation. Although the EU is the leading provider of humanitarian aid and balance-of-payments support to Russia, the Russian authorities frequently harass European companies based there.

When an international crisis emerges, the EU often acts together with the United States, particularly on human rights issues. But sometimes the two disagree. The United States occasionally teams up with Russia and China (neither of which is a Western-style parliamentary democracy) in opposing multilateral solutions to security problems. Brazil, India, and South Africa have on several occasions backed the EU in its desire to tackle security problems by working through the UN. In 2030 the United States is the world's only truly global diplomatic and military power. In the Middle East, which is even more central to the world's energy markets than it was in the late twentieth and early twenty-first centuries, the EU vies with the United States and China for influence. The EU is the biggest provider of peacekeepers to the region, and it has integrated Israel into its single market, while China has the greatest trade and investment ties with many Arab oil-producing states, and the United States has close security partnerships with several governments.

The EU president and foreign minister are respected figures on the international stage, though their peers tend to pity them because the member-states greatly constrain what they can say and do. Outsiders find the EU's "variable geometry"—with different member-states taking part in different policies—baffling, as do many voters within the EU.

WHAT KIND OF MULTIPOLARITY?

This chapter attempts to explain how the EU is likely to shift from where it is today to the kind of organization sketched above. It is obvious to many observers of international affairs in 2009 that power is shifting from West to East and that the world is becoming increasingly multipolar. They see a gradual transition from the hegemonic order of the 1990s, when the United States was the sole superpower, to a more complicated international system in which several powers—including Brazil, China, the EU, India, Japan, and Russia—have weight or the potential to develop it.

Economics—notably the rapid growth of the BRIC (Brazil, Russia, India, and China) economies—is driving this change. According to predictions by the Economist Intelligence Unit, by 2020 the U.S., EU, and

TABLE 5-1. SHARE OF WORLD GDP

Percent[a]

	1995	2007	2020	2030
United States	21.7	19.4	18.3	16.6
China	5.5	10.1	17.7	22.7
Japan	8.3	6.0	4.6	3.6
India	3.1	4.3	6.9	8.7
Russia	2.8	2.9	3.1	2.7
EU-27	24.5	20.8	18.6	15.6
France	3.6	3.0	2.5	2.1
Germany	5.3	3.9	3.2	2.5
United Kingdom	3.4	3.1	2.9	2.5

Source: Economist Intelligence Unit (EIU.com).
a. GDP figures are calculated at purchasing power parity (PPP), a measure that takes account of the lower price level in developing countries. In December 2007 the World Bank's International Comparison Program released new PPP calculations for 146 countries for 2005; China had fully participated in this survey for the first time. The new data suggest that the emerging economies are much smaller than previously assumed—and the new estimate for China is 40 percent lower. The EIU's projections are based on the new estimates.

Chinese economies each will account for just under 20 percent of global GDP, calculated on the basis of purchasing power parity (table 5-1). It predicts that by 2030, the Chinese economy will be the largest in the world, while the relative weights of the U.S. and EU economies will continue to fall. Although much uncertainty surrounds such figures, the trend seems clear.

Of course, military and diplomatic power does not always correlate closely with economic output. At the moment, the United States accounts for almost half of the entire world's defense spending, and it is likely to remain the supreme military power for many decades ahead. But there is little doubt that over the long term, the West (defined as the North Americans and the Europeans) will become weaker relative to the rest of the world. The fact that the current financial and economic crisis began in the West, and particularly in the United States, has only reinforced the perception in many countries that the age of Western leadership is drawing to an end. The main institutions of global governance, such as the UN Security Council, the G-8, and the International Monetary Fund, are steadily losing legitimacy and authority because of the underrepresentation of new powers and the developing world.

Although the trend toward multipolarity is indisputable, the nature of the system that will emerge is not. Two kinds of multipolarity seem plausible: one competitive, the other cooperative; one based on the assertion of national power, the other on multilateral rules and organizations.

The leading nations, or poles, could line up in two competing camps, driven by ideology or some other set of interests, as happened during the cold war. For example, the American author Robert Kagan believes that the underlying political values of the various countries will determine who their best friends are. If his analysis is correct, Russia and China could form an "axis of autocracies," united by their dislike of Western political liberalism. They would face an axis of democracies, consisting of the United States, Europe, Japan, and possibly India.[1]

Most Europeans fear that that kind of balance-of-power politics could create rifts in the emerging international system. They believe that the major challenges of the twenty-first century—such as climate change, energy security, financial stability, migration, and terrorism—require cooperation among all the leading powers, not just some of them. Europeans want to see a multilateral model of multipolarity. There would be shifting coalitions among the poles—and the democratic ones would have a natural affinity for working together—but all would take part in multilateral institutions and treaties and respect international law. As the EU's 2003 European Security Strategy put it: "In a world of global threats, global markets and global media, our security and prosperity increasingly depend on an effective multilateral system. The development of a stronger international society, well-functioning international institutions and a rule-based international order is our objective."

Of the major powers, the EU will always be the biggest champion of multilateralism—since the EU itself is a multilateral construction, the concept is coded in the DNA of its politicians. China, Russia, the United States, and India, by contrast, can easily switch between unilateral, bilateral, and multilateral behavior, depending on each country's perception of which tool best promotes its self-interest.

However, the new international system is likely to be predominantly multilateral. As U.S. power becomes relatively weaker, the argument in favor of its acting multilaterally rather than unilaterally will grow stronger. If the United States becomes concerned about the behavior of other powers, it is more likely to see the case for building strong international institutions to constrain them. As the scholar John Ikenberry puts it: "U.S. dominance will eventually end. U.S. grand strategy, accordingly, should be driven by one key question: what kind of international order would the U.S. like to see in place when it is less powerful?"[2]

Moreover, the world's democratic powers are unlikely to want to form an alliance against Russia and China. Many Europeans and Americans are convinced that engagement is preferable to confrontation, and Western business interests will also push for open and amicable relations with the booming emerging markets. Nor is it likely that India, though a democracy, would want to take part in a Western strategy of containing Russia and China.

And would those two authoritarian states wish to form an axis? Their governments currently have a good relationship and share a common distaste for the "color revolutions" that have led to the emergence of relatively liberal and democratic systems among some of their neighbors. But Russia and China are not natural allies, and there is not much trust between their political elites. Moscow knows that in any close partnership with Beijing, China's economic strength is likely to make it the leading partner, and many Russians fear Chinese encroachment on parts of their territory. China's leaders tend to be dismissive of Russia's economic prospects. [3]

The two powers also have very different views on how to deal with the West. During Putin's second term as president, the Russian leadership often seemed paranoid about the West's intentions, and it sometimes chose to deal with both Europeans and Americans in a truculent and confrontational manner. The tone may be a little softer under President Dmitri Medvedev, but there are few signs that the fundamentals of Russian foreign policy have changed. The leadership of the Chinese Communist Party, by contrast, has a strong interest in avoiding rows with the United States while it focuses on building China's economic strength. It cares much more about its relationship with the United States than its relationship with Russia. China's leaders can be prickly, but because they want their country to be accepted as a responsible power, they sometimes take account of Western viewpoints—for example, on climate change.

Therefore the balance-of-power model of multipolarity does not, at present, seem likely. The European Union itself will have a big influence on how the international system develops. The stronger the EU becomes, the more influence it will have. And it is likely to become stronger, thereby helping to push the international system toward multilateralism.

THE REGIONAL ENVIRONMENT

Do the Europeans really want to shape the emerging world order? Currently, they are divided on that question. In Britain, France, Poland, the Netherlands, and some other EU member-states, many senior figures in the political, diplomatic, and military establishments would argue that the Europeans should try to play an active role in geopolitics (though some British Conservatives would not see much role for the EU itself in such activism). They are firm believers in the idea of humanitarian intervention and in enforcing international justice. They are prepared to send soldiers to places where those soldiers may get shot. And they are willing to spend money on developing diplomatic, humanitarian, and military capabilities.

But many parts of Europe do not subscribe to the activist approach. Political leaders in places such as Austria, Belgium, Germany, Slovenia, and Spain are reluctant to spend money on defense, unwilling to send troops into harm's way, and cautious about the concept of humanitarian intervention. Such countries spend closer to 1 percent of GDP on defense than the 2 percent that those that are also NATO members have committed themselves to spend. They also apply caveats when their soldiers serve on peacekeeping missions, preventing them from using force. In such countries, the public often will oppose the use of force and assume that international problems can be solved entirely through aid and diplomacy. In a nutshell, some Europeans would like to live in a big Switzerland—a country that is peaceful and safe and does not trouble itself with trying to sort out the world's problems.

Between the extremes of Tony Blair's interventionism—Blair sent British forces into battle five times during his premiership—and the big Switzerland thesis there are, of course, several shades of gray. Many countries are divided. Thus, in Italy the political right and the moderate part of the left tend to favor interventionism, while many others oppose it. By 2030, those who want an activist Europe are likely to have won the argument for two main reasons. First, as already discussed, the geopolitical environment will not be reassuring. In the multipolar world of the future, powerful states that are not democratic will wield authority and influence. Europeans will not want to be pushed around.

Second, the EU's immediate surroundings are also highly likely to give cause for concern. The 2003 European Security Strategy highlighted five threats in the European neighborhood: proliferation of dangerous weapons, terrorism, failed states, regional conflicts, and organized crime. It would be foolhardy to predict that organized crime and its links to illegal immigration and drug running are unlikely to be a menace in 2030. The risks of the proliferation of nuclear and other weapons are growing: the safety and security of many nuclear materials that originated in the former Soviet Union remains troubling, while the Iranian nuclear program threatens to set off a wave of nuclear proliferation in the Middle East. In places close to the EU, such as the western Balkans, the Caucasus, and the Maghreb, war remains possible (though by 2030 all of the Balkans is likely to be in the EU). Not much further away, in Afghanistan, Somalia, and Sudan, weak states and civil wars pose dangers to Europe. Jihadist terrorism is far from defeated. Since 2003 one global problem, climate change, has moved up the political agenda, while energy security has become a growing concern for many Europeans.

Also since 2003, Russia has evolved in ways that are troubling, and it is plausible that Russia in the 2020s could challenge the security of some EU states. During the Russia–Georgia war of August 2008, Russia's leaders sent a clear message to the West: Russia is back, it has its own sphere of influence, and, if provoked, it will turn to force as a means of resolving problems. But whether or not Russia becomes a truly great power will depend less on its military capabilities than its ability to tackle its massive economic problems. If it can diversify its economy beyond hydrocarbons, create a business environment that encourages Russian companies to innovate and integrate with the global economy, limit the worst excesses of corruption, and halt its demographic decline, Russia will be a power to be reckoned with. But if Russia's leaders fail to tackle those challenges—and they currently are not doing well with respect to any of them—the EU will have to devote money and time to helping its weak but irascible neighbor.

The area that Europeans regard as their backyard is also likely to widen. The focus of the EU's emerging foreign policy has been mainly the Balkans, the countries that lie between Russia and the EU (Ukraine,

Belarus, Moldova, and the three Caucasus states), the Middle East (with a special emphasis on trying to support the peace process there), and with the launch of the Union for the Mediterranean in 2008, North Africa. But already the EU is actively involved in the diplomacy over Iran's nuclear program; it has sent peacekeepers to Chad and Congo; and it (largely unnoticed) provided €15 billion in aid to Afghanistan over five years beginning in 2003.

To be sure, the EU is not about to become a global superpower. It will not have a lot to say about how to defeat drug gangs in Colombia or to solve the problem of the North Korean nuclear program. And in the event of a U.S.-China conflict over Taiwan, no European country would send troops.

However, partly because of enlargement, the EU will need to focus on an area that is wider than the area that commands its attention today. By 2030 the EU will include all of the Balkans, Switzerland, Iceland, and Norway; Turkey, Ukraine, Moldova, and Belarus probably will be members; and some of the Caucasus countries may have joined. Those neighbors that do not join will develop intimate relations with the EU. So the EU will be closer to troubled areas such as the Middle East and Central Asia. If there ever is a peace to keep between Israel and Palestine, Europe is certain to be called upon to provide many of the peacekeepers, along with helping Iraq and Afghanistan to become peaceful, normal countries. And involvement in Afghanistan will mean that Pakistan has to become a central concern of EU policy.

The EU also is likely to become more involved in sub-Saharan Africa. A growing proportion of its energy will come from West Africa, and political instability in places such as Nigeria, Sudan, Somalia, and northern Uganda has implications for terrorism in Europe. Africa is already becoming more important to the European Security and Defence Policy (ESDP). A peacekeeping force was sent to Chad in spring 2008, security sector reform missions are under way in Guinea Bissau and the Democratic Republic of the Congo, and the EU is giving money and technical assistance to help the African Union provide peacekeepers in Darfur.

One reason why the EU will extend the geographical scope of its foreign and security policy is that the United States is going to assume that the EU can look after the regions around it. The Americans are likely to focus on Asia and the broader Middle East. If there are problems in the

Balkans, Eastern Europe, or North Africa, the EU will be expected to sort them out. And the United States will expect the EU to contribute more than it has to date in places like Iraq and Afghanistan.

It is highly likely that in 2030 some of the world's most dangerous places will lie close to Europe. The EU will have to get its act together as a defender of its own security, because nobody else is going to tackle many of the threats that it may face. The big Switzerland thesis becomes less sustainable with each passing year. Europe will need to become stronger. But how will it achieve that objective?

BUILDING EUROPE'S SOFT POWER

Although the broad trends shaping international relations in the twenty-first century appear to be clear, nothing should be taken for granted. If Europe wishes to ensure that the new world order is something close to the multilateral vision described in this chapter, it will have to work to shape that order—and it will need both hard and soft power. Many Europeans are justly proud of the EU's soft power—its ability to persuade or inspire people to do things through the attractiveness and success of its model—but soft power has its limits. Europe needs to develop its still inadequate hard power. When the Balkans erupted into warfare in the 1990s, the EU's soft power and diplomacy were unable to prevent carnage. That was a big factor behind the birth of the European Security and Defence Policy in 1998.

The European Union should not be complacent about its soft power. Of course, the EU does offer an attractive model—of peace, prosperity, democracy, and liberty—to many other countries, especially its neighbors. But soft power needs to be worked at, just like hard power. In the soft power stakes, the EU is far from being a winner in every area. By most accepted definitions, nearly all the best universities in the world are in the United States. Not surprisingly, the majority of India's best and brightest want to study at U.S. universities rather than in Europe. In some African countries, politicians prefer the Chinese model of development—based on a large role for the state, the protection of key industries, and rejection of external conditions—to Western thinking on development, which is seen as patronizing. Europe, therefore, needs to work at enhancing its soft power. The essential ingredients include the following:

—*A successful European economy*. Despite the current global recession, today's EU includes many successful economies that the less successful can and should emulate. Europe leads or co-leads the world in areas such as international finance (some, though not all, of the skills concentrated in centers such as the City of London will be in demand when the dust of the financial crisis has settled), precision engineering, and luxury goods. But much of the world regards Europe as overregulated and undynamic—a perception that undermines the EU's soft power. Most of the ingredients required for dynamic European economies are well known: an economic reform agenda that gives priority to innovation and a stronger competition policy; new schemes to attract skilled migrants to the EU; liberalization of energy and services markets; and reform of higher education, leading to more autonomous and better-funded centers of excellence.[4] Progress in recent years has been better than many observers have realized. For example, the EU has made steady, if slow, progress in deregulating markets such as those for energy, telecommunications, postal services, and some general services; many governments have reformed their pension schemes to take account of demographic change; and so on. But so long as the recession endures, governments will find it hard to push ahead with painful reforms.

—*An EU that leads the world on climate change*. Europe's determination to tackle carbon emissions contributes to its soft power. But climate change has the potential to create huge rifts in the multipolar world—for example, between powers that back an international system for limiting carbon emissions and those that spurn it. By the time of the inconclusive UN conference on climate change in Copenhagen in December 2009, no other country or bloc had come up with such a serious commitment to act on reducing emissions. But if the Europeans can make a success of their own carbon-trading scheme, persuade the Americans to sign on for a global system, and offer their best environmental technologies to developing countries, they have a fair chance of convincing most of the world to join them in a new system after the Kyoto Protocol expires in 2012.[5] The agreement reached at the December 2008 EU summit suggests that the union is serious about implementing its target of cutting greenhouse gas emissions by 20 percent from 1990 levels by 2020.

—*Continued EU enlargement.* A union that takes in more countries in southeastern or eastern Europe, extending its market, would not only benefit economically. A truly continental union that includes predominantly Muslim countries would have more influence—and would be treated with more respect—in many parts of the world. The EU should make a clear statement of intent to keep its doors open to newcomers. But because enlargement is likely to move slowly and because there are limits to how far EU frontiers can expand, in the short term the union needs a much stronger neighborhood policy. The more politically and economically advanced the neighbor, the more it should be integrated into EU programs and policies. In June 2008, the EU set up the Union for the Mediterranean as a new framework for dealing with the countries to its south. In a parallel move, in May 2009 the EU launched its "eastern partnership," which includes the idea of deep free trade—taking the concerned countries to its east into the single market and removing nontariff as well as tariff barriers. Ukraine is already negotiating a deep free trade agreement. The eastern partnership also offers somewhat easier visa regimes and extra money to promote better governance in the partner countries. But the EU will discover that it needs to make a more generous offer to its neighbors if it wants to influence them.

—*A greater capacity for delivering common foreign and security policies.* This objective requires, more than anything, unity of purpose among national governments. They need to understand that where they have common interests, they often will achieve more by acting together—for example, on policy toward Russia or China. But the EU's institutions also have the potential to make a positive impact on foreign and security policy. At present, the suboptimal institutions that the EU shows to the rest of the world—a presidency that changes every six months and two rival foreign policy bureaucracies in the European Commission and the Council of Ministers—are damaging to Europe's soft power. The entering into force of the Lisbon treaty will help the EU to speak with one voice, when it has a common position on a foreign policy question. The proposed external action service (EAS), based on the merger of those two bureaucracies, should produce the kinds of analysis that will help governments to recognize their common interests and pursue those interests in a more focused and strategic manner. The EU's partners will be grateful for that.

—*More efficient cooperation on issues of justice and home affairs.* Because there is a limit to what individual member-states can achieve on their own, the EU will become much more involved in issues such as counterterrorism, illegal immigration, and organized crime. By 2030 the EU probably will have established an internal action service (IAS), modeled on the EAS. The logic for an IAS will be the same as that for the EAS. Many member-states will not trust the Commission to handle some of the more sensitive aspects of justice and home affairs, such as judicial cooperation and counterterrorism. But they will recognize that the EU institutional system adds value, notably by helping to join up the union's various policies. So they will favor a body that, like the EAS, blends the "community method" with intergovernmentalism. The IAS will take in the plethora of existing EU bodies active in these areas—such as Europol, Eurojust, Frontex (the new border agency), and Atlas (an embryonic counterterrorism network)—whose operations often overlap. Forging them into a single organization would improve efficiency and thereby help to improve the EU's standing among the many countries with which it will engage on justice and home affairs issues.

—*Stable EU institutions.* Institutional reform is of little interest to people in other parts of the world. But the EU's institutional framework does have an indirect bearing on its soft power. If the EU is seen to have ineffective institutions or to be constantly arguing over their design, it will not be taken seriously. And that applies not only to external perceptions of the EU but also to views from within. Euroskeptics in Britain and other member-states have drawn strength from the fact that the EU always seems to be busy with treaty change, institutional wrangling, voting rules, and procedural arguments rather than dealing with real problems in the real world. Now that the Lisbon Treaty has been adopted, treaty change will be off the agenda for at least a decade and perhaps much longer. The EU, its institutions, and its governments are likely to be focused on challenges like climate change, energy markets, and financial stability rather than institutional arguments in the coming decades. That will make the EU more attractive to its citizens and to people in other countries.

—*Strong support for international law.* Europeans sometimes forget that an important source of their soft power is their respect for international law. One reason for the decline in the soft power of the United States in recent years has been its disregard for international law, especially in the first term of President George W. Bush. While many smaller countries support such treaties as a way of limiting the power of large countries, they also are a useful tool for reducing the risk of war. President Barack Obama is already making a point of treating international institutions with more respect than his predecessor did. The EU should be in the forefront of campaigning for the revival or improvement of old treaties—such as the Comprehensive Test Ban Treaty and the Nuclear Non-Proliferation Treaty—and for the negotiation of new ones—for example, a treaty to cut off the production of fissile material. And it should make a point of trying to persuade Russia, China, and the United States to sign on to the International Criminal Court.

—*Reform of global governance.* Many of the institutions of global governance fail to represent the emerging powers adequately, with the result that those institutions are losing authority. One virtue of the economic crisis is that the Western powers have come to accept that bodies such as the IMF and the World Bank must be reformed so that big economies such as China and India have greater weight within them. The G-20, which has begun to meet at the head-of-government level, is already overshadowing the less representative G-8. But much more needs to be done. In order to revive its fading legitimacy, the UN Security Council (UNSC) must become more representative, which means that countries like Brazil, Japan, India, and South Africa have to join. China needs to facilitate that change, but the EU also needs to define its own position on UNSC membership. The EU should take the lead in helping to set up new institutions. One will be needed to manage the global system for curbing carbon emissions, while another should bring together the principal producers and consumers of energy to ensure more stable oil prices. Global institutions cannot be reformed or created without the active involvement of emerging powers such as China and India. The Europeans should urge those powers not to leave it to the Americans, Europeans, Russians, and others to design the new world order.

—*Constructive engagement of the EU with other global powers.* The EU's most important external relationship will remain the transatlantic link. If the EU can show itself to be a useful and effective partner, the United States is more likely to choose a multilateral path. But the same applies to the other polar nations, which the EU will find much more difficult to deal with. If the EU can establish strategic dialogues with the likes of Russia, China, India, South Africa, and Brazil, it will increase the chances that they will support a multilateral system. Those dialogues should focus on difficult issues of common concern, which, if tackled constructively, will help to strengthen global governance. For example, a strategic dialogue with China could focus on climate change, Africa, nonproliferation, global governance, and the maintenance of an open global trading system.[6] An EU that engages other powers and makes a point of searching for common ground with them will be a more influential international actor.

The sources of European soft power are manifold. None will emerge automatically from within Europe's political and economic systems. European leaders will need determination, effort, and vision in order to achieve progress in the various areas discussed above. But in each of them, progress is more likely than not.

BUILDING EUROPE'S HARD POWER

The United States is likely to retain some involvement in European security in the coming decades. That is desirable for Europe: a massive crisis in Kosovo or Bosnia could prove to be beyond the ability of Europeans to handle alone. Nevertheless, the scale and depth of the U.S. commitment to Europe and the regions around it is likely to diminish. In the Balkans, Africa, and, increasingly, the broader Middle East, Americans will expect Europeans to provide not only money, aid, and civilian personnel (as they already do), but also soldiers and military equipment.

The Europeans will need to take on greater responsibility for their own defense.[7] By 2009, the EU had managed, generally with success, two dozen ESDP missions, most of them modest in scope. However, the ESDP has not fulfilled expectations, notably in terms of boosting European capabilities. The world will not take the EU seriously as a foreign policy actor unless it strengthens its defense capacity. The demand for the EU to intervene militarily in its neighborhood is likely to increase, and the intensity of some of the conflicts that it may have to deal with may be serious. So far, deployments of troops under the ESDP have been essentially for peacekeeping. By 2030 the EU is highly likely to be undertaking true combat missions.

The problems that need to be overcome between now and 2030 are well known. Defense budgets have been falling in real terms for twenty years in most member-states, and they are inadequate for the military tasks confronting the Europeans. Worse, much of the money is spent inefficiently, supporting twenty-seven separate defense bureaucracies, large conscript armies that are of little practical use, and an unnecessarily large number of armaments programs. The twenty-seven members spend about €200 billion a year on defense, yet they cannot deploy more than 100,000 of their 2 million men and women at arms at any one time. And ten years after the launch of the ESDP, EU forces are still suffering from serious shortages of equipment. The lack of airlift capacity is a habitual problem; on many occasions, ESDP peacekeepers have been carried to their destination in rented Ukrainian aircraft. The deployment of the ESDP mission to Chad in 2008 was delayed until Russia provided some of the helicopters that EU governments could not find.

There is in the majority of EU member-states a strategic culture that is reluctant to use force and put national forces in danger. European governments also have a poor record of coordinating their civilian and military efforts when reconstructing conflict zones. Agencies charged with development protect their turf against defense ministries and vice versa. The inability of most EU governments to coordinate the work of soldiers with those involved in aid and development has been evident in Afghanistan.

At the EU level, too, the lack of a comprehensive approach to post-conflict reconstruction is evident. For example, during 2005, the first year of the ESDP peacekeeping mission in Bosnia, the general in charge, David Leakey, found that his troops, the EU police mission, the office of EU special representative Paddy Ashdown, and the European Commission were pursuing separate agendas, without much coordination. A related problem is the fact that NATO and the EU have found it hard to work together. For example, the long-running rift between Turkey and Cyprus has prevented NATO from providing military protection for EU policemen in Kosovo and Afghanistan. The fact that the Turkey-Cyprus problem prevents formal contact between the two organizations is damaging to both as well as to Europe's ability to project power.[8]

That is a long list of problems that need to be fixed if the EU is going to be capable of mastering the security crises of the next twenty years—and if it is going to be treated by the United States as a serious partner.

But the problems are all fixable, and by 2030 the EU is likely to be a much more effective military organization than it is today.

In terms of equipment, Europe's armed forces will be much better out-fitted by the 2020s. As a result of projects already under way, they will have Airbus transport planes and refueling aircraft, Typhoon and F-35 jets, unmanned combat aerial vehicles, precision-guided missiles, the Galileo satellite navigation system, and much else. A lot of the new invest-ment in the next twenty years will be in information and communication technology (ICT), probably supplied by commercial ICT companies rather than traditional defense contractors. The Europeans will need to embrace network-centric warfare to increase the productivity of their expensive and scarce soldiers, airmen and -women, and sailors. The investment in ICT will also enable the Europeans to operate alongside the Americans.

Many of the new ICT systems depend on satellites, which are likely to be a growth area for defense procurement. In contrast to most other sorts of military equipment, they are becoming significantly cheaper in real terms. Europeans will depend on satellites not only for communications, listening, and imagery, but also for early warning of missile launches. If, as is quite likely, potentially hostile countries develop ballistic missiles that could reach Europe, EU governments will have to spend money on mis-sile defense systems. They will work with the Americans—and the Russians—to get the most effective and cheapest systems.

Notwithstanding the value of ICT, EU governments will need more deployable soldiers than they have today. The armed forces of the larger EU states are overstretched, and there is little sign that demand for peace-keepers will diminish. That is not to say that the ability to deploy police officers, judges, and aid workers is unimportant; one great strength of the EU is that it can offer a package including skilled personnel, aid pro-grams, and trade opportunities to a zone recovering from conflict. How-ever, any civilians that the EU deploys will need to work in reasonably secure conditions, and security often requires military boots on the ground. By 2030 the EU governments will be able to deploy 250,000 troops on short notice, up from around 100,000 today.

Money is a large part of the problem. Currently the only EU members to meet NATO's 2 percent of GDP target for defense spending are Britain, Bulgaria, France, and Greece. The cost of most sorts of defense equipment is rising much faster than general inflation. To help to meet the likely demand for troops and equipment, the EU should itself adopt a 2 percent target for its member-states' defense budgets. It is not realistic to expect agreement on such a target in the short term, but governments could nevertheless agree to spend 10 percent of their defense budgets on R&D or procurement or both, while adopting the 2 percent target as a long-term objective.

The Treaty of Lisbon includes provisions for "structured cooperation"—the idea that a group of EU member-states could set up their own defense club. Such a defense avant-garde is likely to emerge at some point and could boost European defense. The militarily serious countries would set up a new body under the EU's aegis that would be prepared to undertake combat missions. There would have to be strict entry criteria, based on capabilities—for example, the proportion of troops that are deployable, expenditures per soldier, and the quality of the soldiers' equipment. Those hurdles should be set high enough to ensure that less serious countries could not join. The idea of a defense club, which would inevitably be dominated by Britain and France, should encourage European governments to do some of the things that they have been reluctant to do (spend more money, provide more troops that can deploy at short notice to a distant place, accept common rules on procurement, and so on). When those outside the defense group see its leaders holding regular summits, they might make an extra effort to increase their capabilities so that they can join the club. As the euro did after its launch in 1999, the defense core should act as a pole of attraction to other member-states.

Military reform is essential to improving Europe's capabilities: for any given level of spending, much more can be achieved by militaries and ministries that have been modernized. The United Kingdom has set an example in some areas—for instance, by asking private sector companies to tender for support functions and by merging the logistics organizations of the three branches of the armed service. There is a lot of scope for other countries to catch up. For example, Greece has one of the largest defense budgets relative to GDP in Europe; yet it can deploy less than 1 percent of its troops overseas. Those countries that have not abolished conscription—including Germany, Greece, and some Nordic countries—will have to do so: what Europe needs are professional, mobile troops that are ready and able to go anywhere in the world.

The liberalization of defense procurement markets will allow governments to improve capabilities without spending more money. The small steps that the European Commission has already taken in this regard will have led to a true single market for defense goods by 2030. Such a market is likely to be transatlantic. Protectionism in the U.S. and European defense markets is not going to disappear, but budgetary constraints will force governments to open their markets to outside suppliers. The major EU and U.S. defense companies will have formed transatlantic partnerships by 2030.

A greater emphasis on specialization will have the same beneficial effect. To some extent, this is happening already—the Czechs lead the world in their nuclear, biological, and chemical protection capability, while the Estonians specialize in cyber-warfare. Denmark has considered giving up its air force, and so on. Today, only Britain and France are capable of mounting meaningful military missions on their own, as Britain recently did in Sierra Leone and France did in Ivory Coast. It is highly unlikely that even those two will be able to muster a full range of national military capabilities in 2030. The smaller countries will certainly be specializing much more than they do today.

Pooling of military assets and organizations will also give the Europeans more bang for their buck. There is already a trend in this direction, with NATO running fleets of both early warning radar and ground-surveillance aircraft. The EU will operate its own fleet of transport planes. Pooling will begin in non-sensitive areas, such as maintenance, transport, medical, and catering operations. For example, fighter jets such as the Typhoon and F-35 that several member-states are buying will be serviced at just one or two bases. Many of the EU's "battle groups," 1,500-strong units of rapid intervention forces, already consist of soldiers from more than one country. There will be more pooling of soldiers in multinational units, particularly of personnel from the smaller states and those with specialized skills. This kind of integration will be made a lot easier by the fact that future European soldiers will all speak English.

The EU, like the United Nations and the United States, has devoted less attention to developing civilian than military capabilities. But the EU has established a gendarme force; its police missions have been deployed in places such as Bosnia, Kosovo, and Afghanistan; and a group of its administrators and law officers is playing a crucial role in running

Kosovo. By 2030 the EU will have developed a rapid reaction police capability of 20,000 and a civilian reaction force of 50,000 aid workers, doctors, and administrators, ready to depart on short notice. To make those civilian units effective, the EU will have to do a better job of integrating the work of civilians and soldiers on the ground in conflict zones.

Better coordination also is needed at the top of the pyramid in Brussels. The relevant parts of the European Commission and the secretariat of the Council of Ministers sometimes work at cross purposes rather than together. The new external action service will help, by bringing several parts of the EU's bureaucracy into one institution. But the Commission will still need to ensure that key directorates-general that will not be included in the EAS—such as those responsible for humanitarian aid, development, enlargement, and trade—work closely with the EAS in supporting the EU's various missions.

The ESDP will not become more effective unless the EU and NATO learn to work together much more closely and in a complementary way. President Nicolas Sarkozy's decision to make France a full participant in NATO's military structures promises to set the two organizations on the path to a more constructive relationship. Until he became president, a lot of defense policymakers in France and some in the United States saw the NATO-EU relationship as a zero sum game: what was good for one had to be bad for the other. Cooperation between the two bodies is still undermined by the conflict between Cyprus and Turkey, but when that is resolved, as it is likely to be in the next few years, NATO and the EU will start to do much more together. Each will focus on its core strengths—civilian and smaller-scale military contributions for the EU, large-scale military actions for NATO. Arrangements could be made for NATO to have access to the EU's expertise and tools in civilian crisis management, just as the EU can now draw on NATO assets for its ESDP missions. NATO and the EU must do all that they can to harmonize their procedures and soften the differences in their cultures.

Of all the factors currently weakening European defense, perhaps the most difficult to deal with is the lack of a common and robust strategic culture. "We need to develop a strategic culture that fosters early, rapid, and when necessary, robust intervention," said the original European Security Strategy. "We need to be able to act before countries around us deteriorate, when signs of proliferation are detected, and before humanitarian emergencies arise." Too often that message has been forgotten. NATO's inability to persuade many European governments to send soldiers to the south and east of Afghanistan, where there is a serious war to be fought against the Taliban, is one indicator of the problem. U.S. defense secretary Robert Gates has spoken of a "two-tier NATO" emerging. Exactly the same problem will afflict the EU, if and when it starts to take on more challenging military missions.

The more that EU countries work together on defense, the more the relatively robust strategic cultures of the British and the French should influence their partners.[9] But cultures cannot change and defense budgets cannot increase unless politicians make an effort to explain to their publics that the world is a dangerous place, and that it would be less dangerous if Europeans gave themselves the means to tackle security threats. In recent years very few leaders have made that effort. Yet strategic cultures can evolve, especially when political leaders focus on serious and ever-closer threats.

Much will depend on Germany. Germany is the EU's largest economy. It also is one of the few member-states with a global foreign policy, and it has large and potentially effective armed forces. Unless the Germans are fully committed to the EU becoming a more effective global actor, the union's ambitions will be constrained. Germany has appeared to be less than fully committed. In the past few years, it has shown itself reluctant to work through the EU in dealing with Russia, to support Sarkozy's ideas for strengthening ESDP, and to send troops to fight alongside its allies in the dangerous parts of Afghanistan. The pacifist strain in German foreign policy is, of course, an understandable product of the country's history. German public opinion remains reluctant to see German forces deployed in distant war zones, and that is a major constraint on the freedom of maneuver of political leaders.

But Germany's partners should recognize that it has evolved over the past dozen years, under gentle prodding from allies and occasionally strong leadership from its government. It has abandoned the idea that it should not deploy force beyond the NATO area. German troops have taken part in peacekeeping missions in places like Bosnia, Kosovo, the Democratic Republic of Congo, and Afghanistan. There is every reason to suppose that German attitudes toward the use of force will continue to evolve as World War II recedes in the public imagination. It is true that in recent years some of Germany's policies within the EU have appeared to its partners as nationalistic, but that may be a sign that Germany is slowly becoming a more normal country. If it is learning, like Britain and France, to pursue its national interests in an unabashed manner, it is perhaps more likely, in the long term, to take a British or French attitude toward the use of force.[10]

European politicians need to spend more time debating the circumstances in which it is right to deploy force and the rules under which deployed troops should operate. The scale of the challenges that the EU is likely to face in the coming years will persuade many of its citizens that living in a big Switzerland is not a viable option. But unless politicians lead, public opinion will not shift toward supporting higher defense budgets and a more robust attitude to troop deployments.

THE UNITED STATES AND EUROPE

As argued at the start of this chapter, in 2030 there is unlikely to be an axis of autocracies confronting an alliance of democracies. Unless a single, genuinely threatening security menace appears, the United States and Europe will not be obliged to work together on the key issues of foreign and defense policy. Sometimes their interests will diverge, and often they will need to work with all the leading powers, such as Russia, China, and India, through global institutions.

But the United States and the EU are likely to work together more often, and more closely, than any other two powers. They will do so because of common values, a common history, and a common approach to many economic and political issues. They will understand that if they work together on shared concerns they will have more impact on the world.

In 2030, as in 2009, it is likely that the Europeans will often be urging the Americans to act multilaterally, through international institutions. And the Americans are likely to be telling the Europeans to get their act together so that they can move quickly, decisively, and, when necessary, with force. But the difference will be that in 2030 Europe will have greater relative weight within the transatlantic partnership. A more unified EU foreign policy will give the Europeans more influence in Washington. On purely military matters, the United States will remain much more powerful and therefore the senior partner; on economic and diplomatic issues, the relationship will be more balanced.

The EU and the United States will need to create new institutions for discussing strategic issues. Today's NATO is not the right forum for discussing big strategic challenges, and it will be even less suitable in 2030. By then NATO is likely to be a rather loose global club with a much broader membership than it has today. Its focus will be on peacekeeping, defense diplomacy, and working for common standards, rather than collective defense.

The current diplomacy over the Iranian nuclear problem shows that the key EU states and the United States can cooperate constructively, on an informal basis, on major strategic issues. But the big difficulty in setting up new transatlantic institutions is that the EU has so many member-states, each one of which is, in formal terms, equal. To be effective, a transatlantic structure should involve only the large EU member-states; one that involved every member-state would be as unwieldy and ineffective as NATO's councils. The problem is that the smaller member-states will never agree to cede power and influence to any formal body that involves only big countries. The way forward is probably an informal body that brings together the key European countries and the United States. Some particular crisis will probably spur the leaders concerned to create a new transatlantic structure.

To quote Edouard Balladur, the former French prime minister: "History is starting to be made without the West, and perhaps one day it will be made against it."[11] That disquieting prospect will encourage the EU and the United States to work together more closely than any other powers in the multipolar world of 2030.

NOTES

1. Robert Kagan, "End of Dreams, Return of History," *Policy Review* (Hoover Institution) (August-September 2007).

2. John Ikenberry, "The Rise of China and the Future of the West," *Foreign Affairs* (January-February 2008).

3. Bobo Lo, *Axis of Convenience: Moscow, Beijing, and the New Geopolitics* (Chatham House and Brookings Institution, 2008).

4. Simon Tilford and Philip Whyte, "The Lisbon Scorecard IX" (London: Centre for European Reform, March 2009).

5. Simon Tilford, "How to Make EU Emissions Trading a Success" (London: Centre for European Reform, May 2008).

6. Charles Grant with Katinka Barysch, "Can Europe and China Build a New World Order?" (London: Centre for European Reform, May 2008).

7. In this section I have drawn on some of the ideas that Daniel Keohane and Tomas Valasek promoted in their essay "Willing and Able? EU Defence in 2020" (London: Centre for European Reform, June 2008).

8. Daniel Keohane, "Unblocking EU-NATO Cooperation," *CER Bulletin* 48 (June 2006).

9. See Charles Grant's essay in "The European Way of War" (London: Centre for European Reform, May 2004).

10. Charles Grant, "Unilateral Germany Threatens to Weaken Europe," *Financial Times*, December 5, 2008.

11. John Vinocur, "A Union of the West? Balladur Says It's Time," *International Herald Tribune*, January 7, 2008.

Europe and the United States in 2030

WHAT KIND OF relations will the United States and Europe have in some twenty years? To be able to answer this question we must try to imagine how each of these two entities will evolve, what kind of relations they will have with the "rest of the world," and what the nature of their relationship will be under various future scenarios.

AMERICA: STILL ON TOP?

Numerous American and some European authors have taken to discussing the various possible reasons for the decline of the United States. Among the most cited: deindustrialization due to globalization and outsourcing and competition from emerging economies, which explain the political leanings of the "blue collar" vote during presidential campaigns; the disastrous state of U.S. transportation infrastructure; the colossal debt of Americans as individuals and the United States as a country; the growing dependence on major creditors such as China that this entails; and the shift in power toward Asia, a factor accelerated by the financial and banking crises in 2007–08, demonstrated by the use of sovereign funds from the emerging countries, and symbolized by the creation of the G-20 summit.

None of these weaknesses is insurmountable. The American system has shown throughout its history an extraordinary capacity for regeneration and economic and political resilience. In the global economic crisis of the 1930s, it was the United States, and Franklin Roosevelt, that saved capitalism by regulating it. There are no indications that the United States has lost this capacity—at least not yet. The competitive advantages of the United States remain considerable—no other country compares. It has a willingness to accept leadership and the conviction that it has a "special mission," a demographic vitality from immigration that is unique in the Western world, the persistent global attractiveness of its universities and its investment opportunities, a global currency in the dollar, accumulated geopolitical power, colossal military superiority and cultural soft power, and universal fascination. Even if there are moments of bitter rejection, and even if American hegemony can provoke anger, the United States retains considerable advantages.

It is possible that some sort of global, systemic megacrisis might call into question U.S. hegemony or at least U.S. predominance. But neither the great environmental changes that have already begun, nor the coming energy shortages or the food crisis mean that the United States will soon be supplanted by another power, especially if the United States takes the lead in green technologies. The financial and banking crisis of 2007–09 is American in its origin, but also global in its effect. The United States will suffer from it, but the emerging powers will as well. The hierarchy of powers has not been changed by that crisis, nor has the unstable multipolar evolution of international relations. The rise of Asia, and the emerging countries more generally, began before 2007.

But absent such a crisis, the United States will remain in 2030 the world's most powerful country. No other power, not even China with its population of 1.4 billion, could possibly surpass it in power and influence. However, the United States will certainly no longer be the "hyperpower," a term that I coined in 1998 to characterize a moment without precedent, a moment that brought forth the greatest power that we have ever seen and a nearly unipolar world. This label was analytical, not critical, and it will not apply in 2030. The spectacular emergence or reemergence of several leading powers by then will have brought about a powerful, competitive, and unstable multipolar world. The United States will not be replaced, but it will be challenged and troubled.

So, by 2030 we will see a *relative* economic decline of the United States because of the emergence of other powers, but it will remain preeminent in the military field and will maintain a leadership role, even if it is relative. And the relationship that structures global politics will be that between the United States and China.

A MORE UNCERTAIN EUROPE

The question of Europe's future is even less clear, but it is posed in the opposite way: not, will "Europe" remain a dominant power, but will it *become* one?

Many Europeans are repelled by the idea of power, which they would like to believe obsolete. Indeed, since World War II, they have sought to rid themselves of the necessities, the costs, and the perils of power. They have relied on the "international community," the United Nations, and the protection of the United States. The very French slogan of a "powerful Europe" has not elicited much response. Many Europeans believe in the transforming power of treaties and in the progressive effect of process, such as the process of creating a common foreign and security policy for Europe. A few states, among them France, promote the idea of a "European defense," but in an ambiguous fashion and with modest ambitions. In fact, the strategic reality contradicts this slogan. And the Europeans, because of their histories and particularities, often react in disparate ways to international events. So, in what direction will Europe evolve?

It will not transform into a "United States of Europe," in the sense of the United States of America. Rhetorical references to a United States of Europe, to another Philadelphia Convention, or another George Washington flatter the imaginations of European federalists. Such flights of fancy were perhaps useful to delegitimize nationalism, but they are quite inappropriate for describing the European Union. The Treaty of Lisbon (still in the process of ratification) will probably mark the high point of political integration of the twenty-seven states (or possibly more). In fact, European governments, when and if this treaty is ratified, will not be inclined to reinitiate negotiations for another more integrationist treaty whose ratification would be more than uncertain. They have no reason to do so. *Integration* will therefore not go very far. This is also the meaning behind the recent decision by the German Federal Constitutional Court—integration will stop here.

The European *construction*, on the other hand, will go far. *Construction* and *integration* do not mean the same thing: the first signifies cooperation, the second fusion. Within the stabilizing framework of the Lisbon Treaty, several new common policies will certainly have seen the light before 2030. Immigration policy will have been harmonized and control over immigration increased at the European level. For better or for worse, a common environmental and energy policy will have been developed after the twenty-seven members determine a common position on Russia and surmount their differences on nuclear power, the necessity of which is clear. Other policies or initiatives will surely have been initiated in research, industry, and other areas. Economic policies will finally have been harmonized within the Eurozone, and an economic governance policy will have been implemented or else the euro itself will be threatened.

New pan-European projects will undoubtedly have emerged at the initiative of the European Commission or of a few states interested in drawing on models as diverse as Ariane, Airbus, and Galileo. Such projects may use European community models, and they may avail themselves of the procedure of "enhanced cooperation" and "structured cooperation" as defined by the treaty, or they may use direct intergovernmental arrangements.

More initiatives will undoubtedly have been implemented with regard to European defense. However, this expression does not, contrary to appearances, signify the defense of Europe (Europe is already defended by national forces, by NATO, and, in the case of the United Kingdom and France, by nuclear deterrence). Rather, European defense refers to the capacity of some European countries to intervene jointly on the global level within the framework of peacekeeping missions, and under a UN mandate, or it refers to the few European countries that have defense industries and can justify them (assuming these industries have not been absorbed by transatlantic integration along the lines of the EADS company model).

The harmonization of European foreign policy will presumably have progressed, though this progress will be due more to diplomatic convergence among the larger member states than to a new common diplomatic service. Still, there will not be a *single* global European foreign policy. Europe will remain basically what Jacques Delors has been calling it for years: a "federation of nation states." The center of that federation, the Eurozone, will become denser, but the peoples of Europe will ensure that the nations of Europe do not disappear even as they support common policies within Europe. Only a terrible threat to Europe would produce a greater impetus toward integration, much as the Soviet threat inspired the first round of integration after the war. But what would be the nature of that threat?

Putin's aggressive tone seeks to obliterate the memory of fifteen years of Russian humiliation. Russia poses a serious problem for its neighbors. But it will not pose a global threat, nor will it provoke a new cold war, because it does not seek to challenge the global system, only to increase its weight in that system. Those types of Russian efforts can be effectively managed by intelligent European and American diplomacy, of the type pursued by Barack Obama. In any case, Russia's aggressive tone will not provoke an intensification of European integration—at most it will encourage harmonization of the policies of the twenty-seven toward Russia. And no other major threat concerns Europe directly.

Will all of this progress transform Europe in twenty years into more than just a commercial power? Can reluctant European publics be persuaded that to defend their *interests*, Europe must be a *powerful pole* in a multipolar world rather than just a big Switzerland? Eventually perhaps, but a new treaty will not suffice to change attitudes that are so deeply rooted.

Europe will labor under several handicaps beyond this uncertain will to power. Because Europe's populations are naturally very attached to the various social benefits acquired in the postwar period, Europe will have great difficulty in adapting to globalization. European governments are only able to reform if they are prudent and do so with equity, which is to say that they must combine adjustment and reforms with measures to ensure solidarity, preserve protections (one should not mix up *protection* with *protectionism*), enhance regulation, and boost the economy. Europe faces demographic decline that for reasons of history and social structure will not be fully offset by immigration. The euro faces an uncertain future as well. By 2030 it will either have succeeded in imposing and strengthening itself in Europe and in the world through monetary and economic governance, or it will have been challenged.

The central question thus remains whether or not European public opinion will come to understand the necessity of establishing a European pole of power in a multipolar world. Soft power, norms, and competition policy will not be enough even if they are critical. If they do come around, Europeans themselves will be surprised by their potential. But do the European elites really want a powerful Europe? And will they be able to persuade the public?

THE CHALLENGE OF THE REST

The evolution of the United States, of Europe, and of their relationship to each other will also greatly depend in twenty years on another element: their relations with the rest of the world. "The rest"—the 5 billion human beings who are not Western, many of whom live in countries that are dynamic, emerging powers—will play a much greater role. The emergence of "the rest" will cause a tectonic shift in geopolitics: Western dominance, which has defined the history of the world since the sixteenth century, will be challenged as never before. That challenge represents a massive upheaval in global politics.

It is quite clear that history has not come to an end; on the contrary, "history strikes back," as I noted in an earlier work. The change is not limited to the so-called BRIC countries—a heterogeneous category that includes a China that is rising at a spectacular pace, an India that is emerging more slowly but still powerfully, a Russia that seeks to regain its prominence, and a Brazil that is growing strongly and loudly. Behind them there are twenty or thirty other countries, including Mexico, Thailand, Vietnam, Indonesia, Iran, Turkey, the Gulf states, and even other Arab or African states that we do not usually think of as "emerging," but whose annual growth rate still exceeds 5 percent. This change is already discernible in the colossal growth of sovereign wealth funds, in the dramatic increase in the number and market capitalization of global companies from emerging countries, in the explosion of consumption in these countries, in the economic boom that rising commodity prices have created in producer countries, in the exponential growth of transport, in releases of greenhouse gases beyond the most alarmist predictions, and in the expansion of energy-hungry urban centers. The global economic crisis that began in 2007 will have immense repercussions, and it may slow or modify these phenomena, but it will not make them disappear, nor will it change their general direction. Economic and political relations of all kinds are developing very quickly between all of these new poles, creating new networks that often bypass Western countries. Thus, we now see new relations between China and Africa, India and Africa, China and Latin America, Russia and Iran, and others.

All of this will have given birth in twenty years to a very different world. While the West will retain immense power and influence, it will largely have lost the monopoly it retained for so long, first under the Europeans and then under the Americans. This process is already well advanced. Due to the relative demographic decline of the United States and absolute decline of Europe, the West faces tremendous economic, environmental, and strategic challenges.

How will Western leaders react? With panic or reflection? With force or skill? Will their vision be short term or long term? Relations between the United States and Europe would, of course, be smoother if they would address these problems with the same mind-set. If not, they will be seriously threatened.

People in the West may deny the gravity of these challenges and of these changes. They may place their hopes in the "international community," they may wait for the market, the Internet, high-tech mobile phones, and the homogenization of human behavior on the basis of universal values to create a "flat" earth. But many factors suggest that this is a very optimistic, even unrealistic thesis, characteristic of the type of "unrealpolitik" thinking that has prevailed in the West since the demise of the Soviet Union. Reality will ultimately prevail.

So, what will be the line of conduct of the West toward the world? We can envision two distinct scenarios.

In the first scenario, the West may consider that the emergence of these new powers is only fair or, in any case, inevitable, and that it has already allowed and will allow hundreds of millions of additional human beings to escape from poverty. Western nations may accept that these new powers pose serious energy, ecological, economic, institutional, and strategic problems but that solutions to these may be reached through negotiations. Or they may maintain that it will be easier to deal with these problems if the UN Security Council and G-8 are enlarged and adjusted to new global realities. Because the reform—that is the enlargement—of the UN Security Council is blocked for the moment, the first adaptations will occur in the G-8, which is more malleable since it has no founding text. Indeed, this is what occurred with the G-20 process to deal with the crisis and negotiate new financial and economic regulations, which was launched by the French presidency of the European Union in late 2008. This process was agreed to by all the major powers, including the Bush administration, which was coming to an end and responded with resigned acquiescence, and became a reality soon after. All of these reforms could have been implemented in 1992–93, if the West had been thinking more long term. The West may believe that ultimately the new powers will become the engine of global growth, and that it will be possible to meet the needs of more than 9 billion human beings in a sustainable manner. In this view, the West would still have time to guide the negotiation and implementation of an organized multipolar and multilateral world, as the United States did in 1945, even as the Soviet Union opposed it for forty-five years. The emerging powers would be gradually integrated into this new global order.

But we must be clear: this means that the nations of the West will accept that they must share power. Of course, the implementation of this strategy does not exclude the prudent balancing of relations with one of the poles (for example, China) through close relations with others (for example, India or Japan) as the United States already does. In other words, politics and diplomacy will continue. But they would be conducted without seeking confrontation or pushing non-Western poles into a balancing coalition. On the contrary, this geopolitical transformation must be managed in a non-ideological fashion, over a time span of ten to twenty years, through negotiations and gradual adjustments (such as the recent decision to redistribute voting rights in the International Monetary Fund) and with a minimum of tension.

But things may turn out differently. The concern of the West, its ideology, its divisions, may lead it to a wholly different approach that might be aggressive, would probably be clumsy, and would ultimately be counterproductive. This behavior would divide the West, which would aggravate its problems and make it weaker. Nonetheless, it may be that many in the West, starting with many Americans, will not accept this challenge to the Western monopoly by the Chinese, the Russians, the Indians, and Arabs, among others. They may feel trapped by the 5.5 billion people from these countries and retreat into a defensive bloc, a sort of new "Holy Alliance."

They may believe that this historical upheaval must be countered by all available means: sanctions, boycotts, embargos, ostracism, extraterritorial laws, unilateral interventions, and both "hard" and "soft" power. They may count primarily on a manifest military superiority that is constantly reinvigorated and strengthened, and occasionally used for preventive actions. They may believe it possible to form coalitions as artificial as those enacted by the Bush administration for the "war on terror" to use, for example, against Iran, and make them last even if their inefficiency is evident. They may even try to "isolate Russia," despite the obvious geographical absurdity of that idea. They may be incapable of overcoming the historical antagonism between Islam and the West, and they may even continue to deepen it through counterproductive policies and extreme clumsiness. The model of what to avoid is the Bush administration's policy from 2001 to 2008 toward Iraq, Iran, and the Arab-Israeli conflict, created under the combined influence of neoconservatives, evangelical Protestants, and the Israeli Likud party—as well as, perhaps, President George W. Bush's personal convictions.

The West will possibly also not succeed in effectively prioritizing its objectives toward China, Russia, and others. It may fail to decide who among the emerging powers is a competitor, a partner, an ally, or a threat. Disagreement within the Western camp may arise from numerous other specific problems, such as determining the response to some new initiative of a country perceived as threatening. The West has lost the pseudo-legitimacy that allowed it to determine independently which countries are "rogue," which are part of the "axis of evil," which can be negotiated with, and which deserve sanctions. In this increasingly complex game, one cannot exclude that some crisis will one day take place between a United States, advocating a hard-line solution or even military action, and a China, a Russia, an Iran, or an African or an Arab country (or a combination of all of these) fearful of this approach. "West versus Rest" disagreements may also arise over dependence on energy-producing countries, preferred routes for oil and gas pipelines, control of various key straits, the speed of transformation of unsustainable economies into environmentally sound ones, transfer of sensitive technologies to emerging powers, reforms of the 1945 multilateral institutions to benefit emerging countries, sovereign wealth funds, democratization, and the continuing struggle over the conduct of the "war on terror." And that is without counting unforeseen crises!

The relationship between the United States and Europe will be conditioned by such events, as well as by the evolution that occurs in America and Europe, their relationships with other global powers, and the constructive or dangerous dialectics that they produce.

The only scenario that seems ruled out is a rift between countries on the two sides of the Atlantic. The most likely trajectory would be the continuation of current trends: maintenance of the routine and casual leadership and the strategic predominance of the United States, even if such leadership is eroded and challenged, blind European conformity accompanied by limited protests, occasional commercial and political disagreements, and celebration of the "community of values" matched by numerous divergences of interests regarding societal questions or diplomatic initiatives. This scenario would certainly be reinforced if a "transatlantic free-trade area" was created, as some Americans, echoed by some Europeans, often British, regularly suggest.

What kind of events could undermine these developments?

First, a crisis could deeply affect the transatlantic relationship—one that arose out of a European refusal to support a hard-line American policy toward, for example, Russia, China, or a country in the Arab-Muslim world. The crisis could be triggered by energy or terrorism issues, particularly if the United States chose once again to resort to military force after a deadlock in the Security Council, in essence producing another Iraq crisis. However, this is not Obama's style. European opinion would not tolerate such an approach again. One may object to this scenario by saying that no American president would take the risk of isolating his country, particularly given all the complications created by the new emerging powers. However, we still cannot exclude a negative spiral resulting from a threat to an interest that the Americans consider vital. We need only remember the strong reactions of President Bush and Senator McCain in the spring of 2008 to the rather tepid plans from then senator Obama to extricate American foreign policy from the quagmire of Iraq. The opposite situation, in which Europe would resort to force in the face of opposition from the United States—a replay of Suez involving the whole European Union—is theoretically possible, but it does not merit consideration.

Another important change would be the creation of a real European pole of power. A European pole would not result from the creation of federalist Europe, for which there is very little support among the peoples of Europe. Rather, a European pole could arise out of a methodical effort at convergence among the member states. It would initially involve the large member states, particularly those that have long aspired to a global foreign policy. This convergence would have to cover all of the major areas of potential diplomatic disagreements mentioned, and it would also need to address the method of consultation with Europe's principal interlocutors. Perhaps the spirit of openness of the Obama administration will encourage Europeans to take these steps. The idea of Europe is no longer a problem for the United States, which means we can expect much less drama from the post-Bush United States. Europeans should be able to put this reduction in tensions to good use. Sometime soon, the German chancellor, the British prime minister, the French president, the Italian president, the Spanish prime minister, and all of the others, including the European Union authorities, must accept that although they may visit Washington, Beijing, or Moscow, such visits will require coordination and prior agreement on the messages carried. The strengthening of the powers of the High Representative for the Common Foreign and Security Policy by the Treaty of Lisbon, however useful, will not suffice. This new scenario will require genuine political will, perhaps beyond what European governments are capable of summoning.

Convergence could of course be propelled forward by a crisis, which opportunistic Europeans would use to forge unity under the pressure of extreme events. However, we did not see this during, for example, the Tibet crisis in the spring of 2008. On the issues of the Middle East, the Levant, and Central Asia, the Europeans now have—five years after Iraq—reference points, political positions, pat phrases, and common hopes but no common operational policy. A lot remains to be done.

To preserve close relations and to remain strong in the coming geopolitical storms, Europeans must do more than simply emphasize common values. They must do more than simply prolong the current convenient but unhealthy transatlantic relationship. Europeans who view a strong transatlantic relationship in 2030 as crucial must do more than wish. They must work to build it, not through a delegation of their power to an entirely abstract "Europe," but rather through a "synthesis from the top," or a strategic convergence of the policies of the main member states. This would be the fulfillment of the vision set out by former French prime minister Edouard Balladur, who called for a "Western Union," which implies a true European pole of power.

The Americans, for their part, should not only welcome this European effort as a reaffirmation of the alliance; they should encourage it and prepare for it. The governments of the West could then work together to harmonize their positions. If they succeeded, if they adopted a coherent strategy toward each of the emerging powers, and stuck to it, they might actually manage the changes to come and cope with them intelligently before global upheaval imposes even harsher sacrifices on them. In this way, they could continue to pursue, differently and in the best interests of the new world, the grand Western adventure of the last five centuries. If not, there is every reason to fear for the future of the West, for the protection of its vital interests, and for the maintenance of its values.

Russia in 2030:
A More Attractive Partner
for the EU?

The future is assured. It's just the past that keeps changing.
—Russian saying

*One need only take a careful look at the present and the future
will suddenly appear.*
—Nikolai Gogol

IN THE PAST CENTURY Russian-Western relations have gone through many phases—from World War II alliances to cold war ideological confrontation, from Gorbachev-era euphoria to Putin-era mutual disappointment, from economic partnership to geopolitical rivalry—yet the fundamental tension in the relationship has remained unchanged throughout its tumultuous history.

On one hand, Russia and the West[1] share many things: scientific achievements, geographic borders, and a rich cultural heritage. With the fall of communism and the advance of globalization, the reality of their interdependence has become all the more evident. Indeed, over the past century Russia and Europe have influenced each other more than any other regions of the world. Empires were a common undertaking for both Russians and many Europeans; communist ideology was born in

Europe and applied in Soviet Russia; and today, the global financial crisis, though it originated in the United States, has profoundly affected both Russia and Europe.

On the other hand, real differences exist between Russia and the West. Nowhere is that more pronounced than in the nature of relations between a Russian citizen and the Russian state. Despite talk of "managed democracy," Russia's political system clearly does not aspire to real democracy. Informal practices prevail over the rule of law; freedom of expression and domestic dissent are suppressed through state control of mass media; and political assassinations and abductions continue to make headlines. That poses a serious challenge for the West, which seeks to engage with Russia yet also actively promote the strengthening of democracy and human rights, knowing that a more democratic Russia would also be a more predictable and reliable partner.

Russian foreign policy also is a source of conflict. With respect to strategic culture, Western governments tend to view security threats in terms of intentions and capabilities, while Russians continue to define them in terms of geography and history. Hence Russian policymakers are determined to delineate spheres of influence and support a zero-sum geopolitical competition in the post-Soviet era. Russia has opposed a number of key European policies and initiatives in the region—enlargement of NATO and the EU, humanitarian intervention in Kosovo, the EU's recently launched Eastern Partnership—and frequently complains of Europe's disregard for Russia's political and economic interests in the international arena. In the face of Europe's unwillingness to accept Russia's integration into the EU on Russia's terms, Moscow has begun to reflect on its Asian identity, hoping to find acceptance at least in the East.

The tension between commonalities and differences has led to inconsistent and at times quite antagonistic impulses in Russian-Western relations. Today, global challenges such as climate change, the rise of China and other emerging economic powers, nonproliferation, and the demographic problems threatening to destabilize both Russia and the EU call for greater integration and cooperation. Yet cultural and political differences make integration difficult and even undesirable, particularly so long as it can be achieved only by patching over the gap in fundamental values. Finding a strategy of interaction that exploits Russian-Western rapprochement to the full extent without provoking rivalry and mistrust will be a major challenge in the years to come. In 2030, Europe will have much greater success in striking such a balance, while Russia will remain a complex and at times quite frustrating partner.

U.S.–EU–RUSSIA RELATIONS

By 2030, both international and domestic pressures will have significantly reshaped relations between Russia and the West. In a world in which the United States and China are the prime competitors for global influence throughout Asia and the wider Middle East, those relations will matter less, and the transatlantic community of the twentieth century will be left behind in the new geopolitical paradigm. Future technological revolutions in which neither Europe nor Russia will lead will also transform the security landscape, and the combined military capabilities of Russia and the West, including nuclear weapons and rocket and space technology, will no longer represent the cutting edge. Finally, global energy competition, which will only intensify with the rise of China and India, will further underline Europe's vulnerability while strengthening Moscow's hand and generating more wealth for Russia. The United States will continue to be entangled in the fight for resources and will see much of its power and influence decline as China expands its presence in the Middle East, Africa, and Central Asia.

Although these external factors are important, domestic pressures will have the greatest effect on U.S.-EU-Russia relations. No matter how much hope has been invested in President Obama, there is no doubt that the era of U.S. global primacy ended in the second term of the Bush administration. The impact of a prolonged financial crisis, massive debt (most of it to China and other nondemocracies), and an irreversibly damaged global profile (with more losses to come in Afghanistan and Iraq) will define how the United States is able to position itself in 2030. Europe will remain a critical U.S. partner, but U.S. policies toward Europe will never have the significance that they did throughout the cold war and the 1990s. In light of shifting U.S. priorities, the role of NATO will be further diminished, with NATO becoming only as important as, or even less important than, a new U.S.-EU security agreement. Defeat in Afghanistan will create an existential crisis for NATO and will push the Europeans, who will be the first to leave, and the United States further apart.

As memories and legacies of the cold war fade for the new generations in power, U.S.-Russia relations will narrow in focus, though they will remain problematic. Arms control and disarmament will stay on the agenda, but U.S.-Russia bilateral arms control will be a legacy of the past. As other nuclear powers come to the table, the United States will increasingly be unable to count on Russia as a reliable partner in addressing nuclear proliferation. Similarly, as other countries assert their power and influence in Eurasia—China in Central Asia, Russia and Turkey in the South Caucasus, the EU in Ukraine—the United States will find its role in the region diminished.

In Europe, the future is more complex and uncertain. The first challenge will be to keep European integration alive in the absence of further enlargement and to deepen it in a way that will streamline the decision-making process. Real divisions exist among the member states on how best to engage with Russia, and Russia has long preyed on their disunity by pursuing a strategy of divide and rule. Newer member states, which are likely to become more assertive over time, tend to view Russia as a threat and to oppose increased economic and political integration of Russia with the EU, favoring instead a policy of soft containment. Yet countries like Germany, France, and Italy argue that the best way to ensure a more cooperative and more democratic Russia is through greater interdependence, not less. By 2030, a new institutional framework for EU foreign policy, as mandated by the Lisbon Treaty—having been adopted and fully implemented—will go far to overcome those divisions and provide greater continuity in European policy toward Russia. For Russia, that will mean a reduction in its existing leverage over Europe and an end to the days of "special relationships" and bilateral deals.

Nonetheless, Russia will continue to view Europe as its "natural partner," and by 2030, a renewed EU-Russian partnership will have emerged that is more consistent and transparent. Energy security will remain the central issue. The EU will be increasingly dependent on imports of Russian natural gas, while Russia will seek to attract European investment and trade. By 2030, Europe's demographic crisis, the result of low birth rates, will produce slower economic growth rates across all states and threaten its social security systems. Russia, in contrast, will continue to see higher economic growth than the EU average and gradually will catch up with many of the EU's mid-level economies. Closer economic relations between

Russia and the Central European states will help to overcome political and historical problems between Russia and some former members of the Warsaw Pact. And with neither Ukraine nor Turkey succeeding in obtaining EU membership, Russia and the EU will be able to develop closer cooperation over the Black Sea region and to some degree in the Caucasus. More Russians will be residing in Europe, doing business there, and traveling there to study or to work. The question remains, however, whether Russia in 2030 will be a more attractive partner for a united Europe.

RUSSIA IN 2030

Although delivering a credible forecast of political and economic conditions twenty years into the future is difficult, Russia's recent track record makes it easier to speculate. In the years following Gorbachev's perestroika, it has become clear just how slowly and painfully systematic change proceeds in Russia. Politically, economic growth and stability have come at the cost of civil liberties, pluralism, and diversity. Corruption is widespread, and the rule of law is weakened. A network state, dominated by a loyal and corrupt bureaucracy, has replaced political institutions, and although the middle class is growing, it does not aspire to a political role. In the realm of foreign policy, Russia has moved from a cold war ideology to a pre–cold war mindset, seeking to reassert its sphere of influence among neighboring states and drive the West away from its periphery. Russia has irritated the United States and its allies by sending warships to the Caribbean and strategic bombers to the fringes of NATO airspace. Although much reduced from Soviet times, the Russian army remains essentially Soviet in its structure, doctrine, and threat perceptions.

Economically, Russia has made strides, though they remain fragile, particularly in light of the current global economic crisis. In 2007, Russia's GDP finally regained its 1990 level. The country has acquired enormous wealth, largely due to high commodity prices, but that wealth has been slow to percolate from the elite to other strata of society, from Moscow to other regions, and from energy to other sectors of the economy. The aftermath of the global economic crisis threatens to further weaken Russian macroeconomic stability. Russia will have to spend its significant resources, in gold reserves and in its stabilization fund, to prop up the economy in the face of growing pressures on the ruble and accelerated capital flight. And despite a decade of strong economic growth, the Russian energy sector, the backbone of the economy, still suffers from underinvestment, mismanagement, and technology shortages—and will continue to do so as long as it remains in the hands of the state. On top of all that, Russia suffers from a continuing brain drain, aging infrastructure, and reduced capacity for innovation, all of which only further compound its problems.

Will those trends continue in 2030? Or will Russia find a way to stem and even reverse the tide of authoritarian rule and increasing domestic and economic pressures? In most cases, Russia will continue on its current course, though in some areas the trends will reach more dangerous levels and others will to a certain extent correct themselves.

Economy

By 2030, Russia's economy could quintuple in absolute terms and overtake the German, French, Italian, and British economies in size. Even with the current global financial crisis, Russia's GDP will continue to grow moderately and per capita GDP will increase even more significantly as the population declines as a result of low birth and high death rates. Moreover, Russia will have overcome the impact of the economic crisis of the 1990s and witnessed a steady decrease in poverty levels. In turn, a stronger middle class will develop, and by 2030 it could even exceed 30 percent of the population.

Economic growth in Asia will help Russia develop its Far East and diversify its foreign trade partners to include Asian as well as European countries. Russia will develop a stronger manufacturing base, and the financial sector will undergo consolidation as a result of the prolongation of the current financial crisis. The crisis will also diminish the power of Russia's oligarchs, creating an opportunity to dismantle their post-1990s economic empires. As those monopolies collapse, the competitiveness of Russian companies will gradually increase. The state will demand part of their assets in exchange for financial assistance and then privatize the companies later.

Despite such gains, Russia will continue to lag behind most of the world's developed economies in producing domestic socioeconomic stability, particularly with respect to encouraging innovation and modernizing its aging infrastructure. Russia's ability to overcome those challenges will once again depend on both international and domestic factors. On the international front, the world price of oil and gas will be critically important to Russia. The Russian economy will continue to depend on commodity exports and require foreign investment to expand production, though both will be suppressed for a significant time in the aftermath of the global economic crisis. Foreign investment will not be readily available beyond 2020–30, as the Russian domestic consumer market shrinks and other major economies in Asia, Latin America, and even Africa continue to rise.

Nevertheless, the most significant challenges in determining Russia's future economic growth will be domestic, including the need for economic diversification, declining demographic trends, ineffective corporate governance, corruption, weak property rights and rule of law, and the lack of effective public-private partnerships for economic development. Russia's attempts to diversify the economy, which failed during the time of high commodity prices, will have even less chance of success once oil prices fall and remain low. As a result, Russia will struggle with underdevelopment, capital flight, and growing income inequality. Private sector resources will be limited, and the state will be even more determined to drive economic development through state intervention.

Between 2015 and 2030, the Russian economy also will be preoccupied with costly projects to modernize and replace Soviet-era infrastructure, which by that time will have deteriorated and will be vulnerable to major accidents. By 2010, 70 percent of Russia's ports and 80 percent of its airport infrastructure will need to be replaced, and most of its aircraft and transport ships will have exceeded their service life. Russia's electric grid and utilities will also be in urgent need of modernization, as will its railways, which have been neglected for decades and are critical in supporting economic development, especially the development of new oil and gas fields. Russia is planning to spend around 4 percent of GDP (around $7 trillion) for modernization of its infrastructure between 2009 and 2030. The focus on infrastructure modernization and other public sector investment is intended to help overcome the current financial crisis as well as create jobs and strengthen the country's economic cohesion. However, those aims may not be achieved because of shrinking state reserves, limited private investment (which was expected to cover 60 percent of cost), and the development of alternative energy transit routes through Central Asia and the Black Sea regions.

Energy

Russia will remain an important global exporter of commodities, particularly natural gas, over the next fifty years. By 2030, however, Russian oil production will likely experience some decline. Many sources believe that Russian oil production has already peaked and will fall quite dramatically over the next decade. Even in the best-case scenario, output will increase only marginally, from 490 million tons in 2007 to around 530 million tons in 2030. At the same time, domestic consumption is expected to increase from 95 million tons of oil equivalent in 2005 to around 126 million tons in 2030 or 109 million tons if economic growth remains moderate.

Russia's gas reserves are the largest in the world and, unlike its oil reserves, remain largely undeveloped. Russia's gas production is expected to grow from just over 600 billion cubic meters (bcm) today to more than 900 bcm in 2030. Although many of the existing Gazprom fields are being depleted, new fields including the giant Shtokman gas field can start producing by 2020. In order to develop new fields, more than $1.9 trillion in investment is required as well as technology sharing and development on a number of especially complex projects. Much of the investment will come from Western international energy companies. However, investment in lucrative but expensive energy projects in Eastern Siberia will come from state companies in China, India, and other Asian states. During that time, Russia's domestic gas consumption also will increase, from 128 million tons of oil equivalent in 2005 to between 184 and 199 million tons in 2030. With concerns mounting over Gazprom's ability to meet its domestic and export obligations, that increase in consumption will pose a challenge, particularly in the medium term before new fields are developed.

In 2030 Russia's trade, particularly its gas and oil exports, will be greatly diversified. While most of Russia's natural gas exports will continue to flow westward to Europe, oil exports to Europe will shrink, especially as the volume of exports to Asia grows once Sakhalin production comes on line and the East Siberian Pacific Ocean pipeline becomes operational. Russia's position as the key gas supplier also will be significantly eroded once Iranian and Turkmen gas exports to Europe rise and expansion of liquefied natural gas (LNG) suppiles makes gas a globally tradable commodity. And although Gazprom's monopoly over gas exports will be broken, the Russian state will continue to exercise strong control over production and exports.

Political system

Although Russia's economy will look significantly different twenty years from now, it is unlikely that the political system will undergo any fundamental change. In 2030, Russia will still be essentially an authoritarian state with democratic symbols, such as elections, and little genuine balance of power or democratic accountability of the ruling regime. Vladimir Putin or his proxy will be elected president in 2024, with substantial popular support. Bureaucracy will continue to form the power base for United Russia, the major political party, which will remain the instrument of the powerful executive.

The rise of the post-Soviet generation will not translate into either elite or popular demands for democratic institutions or political pluralism, for reasons discussed below. With the decline of the Communist Party, driven largely by the aging of its popular base, some form of a socialist party and a liberal party will contest the legislative elections, but neither will be able to gain any significant share of the votes or any real degree of power.

Likewise, the consolidation of the bureaucratic-capitalism model will undermine chances for a successful anticorruption program and the establishment of viable state institutions such as an independent judiciary or representative regional governments. The system of appointing regional governors is likely to remain in place, and the powers of regional governments will continue to be curtailed by fiscal and political means. Russia's middle class—which represents the only potential hope for political reforms from below—will remain largely dependent on the state and dominated by beneficiaries of state capitalism rather than private entrepreneurs.

Russia's ability to avoid democratization in the age of globalization, with instant communications and virtual civil society, is linked to the fact that its elite, including the majority of those in the new post-Soviet generation, do not see democracy as the fundamental goal of their country. The first and second post-Soviet generations, which grew up in the 1990s and the first decade of the twenty-first century, are cynical and well-adjusted to a system with no rule of law, no accountability, and no democratic choices. They are much more content with a system of state patronage that guarantees stability through corruption and informal practices while also generating personal wealth. Their attitudes are unlikely to change even with the fallout from the global economic crisis and a state that is unable to produce greater wealth. It will take generations before respect for the rule of law is entrenched in society and the Russian people learn to demand free, competitive elections and to trust their politicians.

Demography and society

For Russian society, which survived through the Soviet period, the collapse of the state in the 1990s, and Putin's revival, the third decade of the twenty-first century will be much less traumatic. With no major upheavals on the horizon, there will be general adaptation to and acceptance of the post-Soviet realities, yet the underlying trends within the society will continue to raise concerns.

First, the Russian population is set to decline considerably, from 142 million in 2007 to around 100 million in 2050, or 120 to 130 million in 2030. In 2007, Russia had the seventh-largest population in the world, but by 2025, it will drop to seventeenth place. The population decline will be accompanied by the aging of the population and the reduction of the working-age population, which is the essential driver of any economic development. The Russian government has been unable to address Russia's peculiar phenomenon of hypermortality, which consistently shows higher death rates among the Russian working-age population—three to five times higher for men and two times higher for women—than rates in other countries with the same level of economic development. Government efforts to stop population decline by increasing birth rates are unlikely to be successful. On top of that, the dramatic rise in drug use and associated cases of HIV/AIDS in recent years will produce disastrous results over the next decade and will be largely ignored by Moscow.

Second, countrywide demographic projections show an impending change in the composition of the Russian population. Russia will witness significant increases in its non–ethnic Russian population, particularly its Muslim population in the North Caucasus and throughout Russia. In 2002, there were 14.5 million Muslims in Russia and Muslims constituted a majority of the population in seven regions of the Russian Federation. Today, the highest population growth is registered in predominantly Muslim regions of the North Caucasus (the highest fertility rate has been observed in Chechnya, with 2.9 children per woman), while in predominantly Russian-populated regions of European Russia, the population decline is predicted to be especially sharp. This trend coincides with growing radicalization of Islamic groups as younger generations of Muslims are prevented from practicing their religion freely and with a growing number of migrants coming to Russia from Central Asia. With Uzbekistan and Tajikistan expecting a population increase of 1.5 times current levels by 2050, these trends are likely to continue, especially as Russia seeks out migrants to compensate for its own demographic decline. Moreover, migration from East Asia, in particular from China, tends to be viewed with suspicion by Russian leaders, who have concerns over Russia's territorial integrity in the Far East. All of these changes could lead to growing nationalism and xenophobia within Russian society, which in turn could provoke interethnic violence and instability and prompt further tensions in the North Caucasus region, particularly if economic opportunities are limited and the middle class continues to experience a decline.

Military

Russia's negative demographic trends will have a direct impact on its military capability. Declining birthrates mean that Russia will be unable to sustain a large conscript army in 2030. Statistics show that in 2007 the share of children from birth to fifteen years of age constituted only 16 percent of the population (the figure was 24.5 percent in 1989) and the number of children of each age from birth to five years was approximately half the number of eighteen-year-olds. In other words, in fifteen years the pool of conscript-age males will be reduced by half. Russia has announced a new plan to abolish conscription by 2030, gradually replacing it with a smaller, largely professional army. That in turn will necessitate fundamental changes in the organization and doctrine of the Russian armed forces as well as a new Russian defense strategy. Yet, past experience with professionalization leaves little room for optimism that the target will be met. However, such restructuring could force the military to concentrate more on real threats in the Caucasus and in Asia, rather than worry about NATO and the United States.

The problems associated with the modernization of Russia's military are not limited to manpower. Equally important are the aging weapons system and declining defense industry. For many years Russia's defense industry has been surviving on the export of weapons—there has been no significant domestic procurement. Even Russia's newer weapons, produced in small quantities, are based on Soviet-era technology. The 1990s crisis in the defense research establishment left a major gap in specialist engineers and weapons designers, which means that Russia's future capacity to produce next-generation weapons will be significantly limited. In 2008, only 20 percent of Russia's weapons could be considered modern. Given the shortfalls of the defense industry, a major modernization effort could lead to closer cooperation with European counterparts like EADS (European Aeronautic Defence and Space Company).

For years, Russia sought to compensate for the decline in its conventional weaponry with a growing reliance on nuclear weapons. However, by 2030 Russia's nuclear deterrent will have to be completely modernized and reduced to less than 1,700 warheads, as it is unlikely that the service life of Soviet-era nuclear weapons can be extended beyond 2020 and the production of new systems—like Topol ICBMs—will remain limited (it currently stands at about ten a year).

Although Russia will retain its nuclear capability, its nuclear deterrent will be far more limited in 2030. That could create a new window of opportunity for rethinking Russian-Western strategic relations and developing closer interoperability between Russia and Western forces, particularly if Russia succeeds in implementing its reform plans to produce a fully professional, modernized army ready for multinational operations and possibly equipped with elements of foreign weapons systems.

North Caucasus

In 2030, with the decline of NATO and China's worrisome but inevitable rise, Russia's most urgent security threats will continue to come from within. Despite Russia's declared victory in the decade-long war in Chechnya, the North Caucasus will continue to generate security challenges—radical Islam, interethnic conflict, new forms of separatism—and could even result in the start of a new war.

First, the radicalization of the new generation of Muslims in the Caucasus, which has been well under way since the 1990s, has spread across the entire North Caucasus region. The brutality of Russian and local law enforcement agencies, poor governance on the part of Moscow-appointed leadership in ethnic republics, lack of attention to the spread of Russian nationalism, and xenophobia with respect to the Muslim population will continue to fuel radicalization. In addition, the nature of radicalization will be transformed as the Muslim opposition moves from individual protest to organized protest in the form of youth jamaats. The jamaats will operate across the region, though they are concentrated in Daghestan, Karachai-Cherkessia, Chechnya, and Kabardiano-Balkaria, and they will benefit from globalization, which offers them links to global jihadi groups. The lack of economic development, poor education, and absence of social mobility within Caucasian societies will further heighten societal tensions and make them more entrenched and widespread. As a result, Russia will face constant violence and terrorism from groups operating both in individual republics and increasingly across the North Caucasus region as a whole. Repressive responses from Russian authorities, which are unlikely to change in 2030, will only make the problem worse and increase the number of young Muslims engaged in violence.

The second challenge will come from unresolved interethnic conflicts in the North Caucasus. The Ossetian-Ingush conflict is likely to further escalate after Russia's recognition of South Ossetia and its de facto incorporation into Russia. Other conflicts could emerge between Chechens and Ingush, particularly if the idea of reunifying Chechnya and Ingushetia is realized. Similarly, interethnic violence in Kabardiano-Balkaria, where the two groups are increasingly separated into monoethnic communities, could also threaten to destabilize the region.

Today, separatism in the North Caucasus has largely been crushed—a result of Russia's brutal suppression of Chechnya and even more substantially by a popular backlash against the leaders of the ethnonational étatist projects of the 1990s, who eventually sold out to Moscow or used their leadership positions for personal gain. Over the next twenty years, however, new leaders could emerge who can once again win popular support at a time when Moscow is increasingly reluctant to modernize its approach to the North Caucasus. One such challenge could come once again from Chechnya if Moscow attempts to remove the current leader—Ramzan Kadyrov—or if he is killed. Another possible movement could come from the powerful Cherkessian community, with considerable support from its diaspora. Russia's recognition of Abkhazia, which could become the first state dominated by a closely related ethnic group (Abkhazians and Cherkessians are part of the same ethnic community), has reinforced Cherkessian nationalism. Finally, Daghestan, with its geographic location, historic Islamic roots, and continuing tensions among multiple ethnic groups, could also represent a major source of conflict with Moscow in the not-so-distant future.

Russia's predominant responses to the challenges in the North Caucasus will continue to be the use of force, repression, and political domination. Those tactics are likely to generate more instability but unlikely to produce another major war, which would be a matter of concern for Russia's Western partners.

FOREIGN POLICY

Like Russia's economic future, the future of Russia's foreign policy is closely linked to domestic development. In 2030, that policy will be shaped more by Russia's experience in the four decades of its post-Soviet transformation than by its Soviet legacy. Russia will continue to aspire to a great power status, but to achieve that status it will have to rely on its own resources rather than its history as an imperial power or superpower. With the new post-Soviet generation replacing Russia's political and economic elite, its relations with neighboring states will undergo a fundamental transformation. Because this generation has, by and large, little or no experience in post-Soviet Eurasia and because of further deterioration of post-Soviet economic links, Russia's ambition and capacity to retain strategic influence in its near abroad will diminish. That in turn could lead Moscow to adopt a more realistic foreign policy agenda and a more stable pattern of engagement. Moreover, such a transformation could also open opportunities for greater cooperation with other regional powers—including China, the EU, and the United States—in pursuing economic development and addressing complex global issues such as terrorism, climate change, and energy security.

By 2030, Russia will have been living for two decades in a world in which Asia's rise becomes increasingly apparent. Russia can benefit significantly from that rise because of its geography and mostly positive relations with the Asian powers. However, its ability to compete with China and India—both economically and, increasingly, geopolitically— will decrease. Russia could assert its role as an Asian power by increasing its energy exports to Asia, but that could be difficult to do given the limitations posed by its production volume and costly export infrastructure. On the other hand, Asian states are likely to influence Russia both through investment and migration. Undoubtedly, one of the more difficult long-term challenges for Russia will be to adapt its domestic and foreign policy strategies to accommodate China's projected rise. In 2030 Russia's economic dependence on China could increase, while China develops strategic ties with some of Russia's closest allies in Central Asia.

Russia-U.S. relations, as stated earlier, will remain important but limited to a number of key issues, such as strategic arms control and nonproliferation—or post-proliferation if the Nuclear Nonproliferation Treaty collapses. The United States is unlikely to develop close economic ties with Russia either in energy trade or investment, and it is equally unlikely that Russia and the United States will cooperate vis-à-vis China's global and regional posture. Similarly, in the Middle East, which will remain the key preoccupation of Washington for decades to come, Russia's role will remain weak at best.

IMPLICATIONS FOR EU-RUSSIA RELATIONS IN 2030

As Russia struggles to address its domestic challenges, sustain its economic growth, and realize its foreign policy ambitions, it will look increasingly to the EU as a long-term partner. In 2030, Russia's proximity to the EU will offer new opportunities at a time when the EU's own global role declines and the transatlantic community of the twentieth century struggles to sustain itself in an increasingly multipolar world. However, the two sides will still have to learn how to accommodate their strategic and political differences and come to terms with their growing interdependence.

Between 1990 and 2005, relations with Russia were secondary to the EU's historic enlargement process and the EU treated Russia as just another transition country in the East. To be fair, it was difficult to give undemocratic and unilateralist Russia priority when other states were much more open to accepting a relationship with the EU based on one-way integration and the adoption of EU norms, values, and standards. Russia was reluctant to integrate with the EU on those terms and tried hard to ignore the EU's expanding role, opting instead for selected partnerships with some of its individual members. Although Russia generally treated EU enlargement more positively than NATO enlargement, the admission of Central European states was met with greater suspicion by Russia and further complicated the EU-Russia partnership.

In recent years, Russia's newly found assertiveness, culminating in the August 2008 war with Georgia, prompted many of the EU's members to view Russia as a troublemaker with whom only a minimalist engagement could be advanced. Moreover, the EU has moved to promote closer ties with Russia's neighbors, such as Ukraine, Georgia, and even the Central Asian states.

The 2010–30 period will be better for EU-Russia relations than the two decades that precede it. The best-case scenario could look as follows. As Russia's demographic decline produces a visible economic impact and its oil and gas production wanes, its economic relations with Europe will begin to be transformed. Between 2010 and 2020, as a result of the global economic crisis, falling oil prices, and gradual changes in relations between Russia and the Central European states, relations between Russia and the EU will begin to follow a more pragmatic and predictable pattern. With both sides focused on rebuilding their economies and resolving social problems, the economic agenda will emerge as the primary basis for a rapprochement. Russia will remain the key gas supplier to Europe as some of its major pipeline projects—such as the North Stream and parts of the South Stream—become operational.

Moreover, by 2030 Russia-EU relations will no longer focus on the common neighborhood, as the previous decade will establish a modus vivendi under which zero-sum perceptions of EU and Russian engagement with post-Soviet states will subside. A multispeed economic integration of post-Soviet states with both the EU and Russia will become a fact of life, with no prospects for political integration with either. The EU will start to play an increasingly important role in Eurasia, including western members of the Commonwealth of Independent States (CIS), the Black Sea region, and to a lesser degree Central Asia—where China will significantly strengthen its economic engagement. However, the focus will no longer be on membership, but on finding ways to promote economic stabilization and developing closer trade ties with the EU. Regional conflicts in CIS will remain "frozen," with neither Russia nor the EU able to achieve sustainable resolutions of conflict. The rise of China and greater destabilization in wider Central Asia will increase Russia's concerns over its eastern frontiers and encourage closer EU-Russia cooperation.

Another source of increased EU-Russia cooperation will be in the area of global peacekeeping operations, including in Africa and the Middle East. Russia and the EU will adopt a visa-free travel regime and promote greater human exchange while increasingly competing for qualified migrants from former states of the Soviet Union. Tensions over Russia's political system, however, will remain, with continuing dialogue on human rights and political freedoms yielding no significant results. Similarly, competition over energy resources in the Caspian region will continue because the EU will be able to bypass Russia and secure supplies from Eurasia while Russia will retain control of other gas export routes from Central Asia. The EU and Russia will develop closer ties on such issues as climate change and the environment, focusing on the impact of melting permafrost in Siberia and reducing the flaring of Russia's natural gas as Russia struggles to meet its 2011 target for stopping all flaring. Tensions over the Arctic will be addressed through multilateral meetings including other global powers.

A number of factors could make a positive scenario more realistic and strategic. The first includes areas in which the EU and Russia will develop greater interdependence—the most important, of course, being energy. Energy will remain the key foundation for EU-Russian economic cooperation. In 2030 EU demand for natural gas will exceed 800 bcm, with

Russia, as the largest and geographically closest producer, continuing to provide a large share of it. The EU will compete with Asia over Russia's gas supplies and over investment in and development of Russia's new gas reserves. Under those circumstances the creation of a Russian-European energy union could produce a win-win scenario for both sides—by increasing Russia's production and guaranteeing the EU's supplies—and could realistically be put on the agenda. The major stumbling blocks—related to Gazprom's monopoly, liberalization of EU energy markets, liberalization of Russia's domestic gas market, and reduction of Russia's state control over the energy sector—will remain if they are not addressed in 2020–30, the "post-crisis decade."

The second set of factors involves technology and innovation, both of which could form another basis for closer economic ties. In 2008, Russia's capacity for innovation trailed that of most developed economies. However, by 2030 that is likely to change as technology companies emerge as a vehicle for sustaining Russia's economic growth at a time of depressed commodity prices. Moreover, as a result of greater investment in educational exchange between the EU and Russia during 2010–30, Russia and Europe will be ready for increased cooperation following a new wave of technological revolutions affecting the energy, space, and public health sectors.

Third, the EU and Russia also have common interests with regard to environmental concerns such as climate change, water resources, and nuclear waste. The EU's ability to meet its greenhouse gas reduction targets after Kyoto timelines will be linked to its ability to replace coal with natural gas or nuclear power as its source of energy; cooperation with Russia, therefore, could help the EU achieve its targets. Moreover, concerns over the impact of global warming on significant parts of Russia's northern population could help to consolidate Russia's support for tighter measures to reduce emissions.

The fourth set of factors is related to demography and migration. By 2030 both Russia and the EU will struggle with demographic decline and an aging population. Both will need to increase immigration to promote economic development and to sustain welfare payments to the elderly. While Russia and the EU could compete for qualified migrants from Eurasia, a better solution would be to develop closer cooperation on regulating legitimate migration flows and combating illegal migration—an issue that is likely to remain significant beyond 2030.

Fifth, security policy offers another opportunity for effective collaboration. As the EU develops a stronger institutional identity and increases its ability to address regional and global security threats, it will seek partners to share the burden of some its long-term missions. Russia, which by 2030 aims to transition to a fully professional, modernized, and deployable army, will still prefer the EU to NATO as a partner in joint operations, with the possibility for joint missions in Nagorno-Karabakh, the Middle East, and Africa.

Despite the considerable potential for closer relations, significant challenges will remain. Russia's peculiar political system, which is unlikely to make any real advances toward democratization by 2030, will continue to be the major obstacle for EU-Russian strategic rapprochement. However, by 2030 the EU's attitude toward Russia is more likely to resemble its current attitude toward China than its attitude toward Uzbekistan. Economic, environmental, and even security cooperation could proceed, even under essentially divergent political systems. Russia's authoritarian regime was a major source of concern in the era of democratic revolution across Central and Eastern Europe, but it will become less urgent two decades after the end of that era. That, of course, does not mean that other states, like Belarus or Kazakhstan, will reject a more pluralist system over the next twenty years. Yet such developments will not represent a strategic trend in Eurasia, where most post-Soviet regimes will maintain a variety of authoritarian systems. The key question will be whether the EU will accept Russia's political arrangements or seek to promote change. In 2030 Russia could once again be ready for such change—not through a democratic revolution but through a gradual erosion of the regime's legitimacy through grassroots pluralism, driven in part by diversity, a growing middle class, and divisions within the ruling elite. The EU should seek to influence that process at the margins and embrace its progress with a promise of closer integration with Russia should democracy succeed there.

Another key difference between the EU and Russia will be their attitudes toward multilateralism. In 2030 Russia will remain essentially a solo player on the international scene. The EU, on the other hand, which is multilateral in nature, will become increasingly so as its integration deepens. That asymmetry will pose a continuing challenge for EU-Russian cooperation over the long run. By 2030 Russia should develop a better understanding and acceptance of EU institutions while continuing to pursue bilateral relations with its member states. Such a change is not likely to come from EU-Russian cooperation but from Russia's participation in other regional organizations such as the Shanghai Cooperation Organization, in which it will have to adjust to growing competition with China. However, Russian political integration will be impossible as long as Russia remains obsessed with sovereignty and unable to develop effective instruments and habits for consensus building.

In order to foster greater cooperation, the EU and Russia will also have to overcome difficult historical legacies. In particular, the legacy of EU enlargement during the post-Soviet era has become a real factor in EU-Russia relations as many new EU member states seek to transfer their historic grievances toward Russia to the EU-Russia agenda. Those concerns will remain important even in 2030, when the post-Soviet generations enter politics in both Russia and the Central European states. In the absence of democratic accountability, Russian political elites will rely on appeals to patriotism as a source of legitimacy, preventing any genuine discussion about the Soviet legacy from taking place in the current political arena. However, normalization of Russia's relations with its Western neighbors should proceed on the basis of pragmatic political and economic interests while leaving some room for addressing difficult historic problems to the next generations.

Russia and the EU also differ in their attitudes toward diversity within their societies. In 2030 the EU states will become more diverse because of migration, integration, and the decline of religion. In Russia, the trends are more controversial. On one hand, its demographic trends point to greater diversity, with the share of non–ethnic Russian and non-Christian populations increasing. On the other hand, the growing influence of the Orthodox Church and widespread xenophobia and intolerance of minorities could generate social tensions and amplify Russia's demographic challenges. Russia should learn from Europe how best to accommodate diversity, and it is in Europe's interest to engage Russia on these issues while promoting tolerance by example, by increasing human contacts, and by encouraging interfaith dialogue with Russia.

Finally, for centuries Russia's relations with Western and Central Europe have been intimately linked to their geographic proximity. Yet in 2030 the EU and Russia have to find ways to extend their cooperation beyond issues of concern only in their common neighborhood. In strategic terms, healthy relations between Russia and the EU can emerge only if they find ways to engage globally and to view each other as essential partners in addressing global concerns. Such a transition will occur naturally as both Russia and the EU develop their footprint in the increasingly multipolar world. Moreover, they will learn to cooperate with or without the United States. While the EU already has demonstrated leadership on such global issues as climate change and development, Russia has yet to find its niche and develop the capacity to become a force for good in the world. It is in the EU's interest to encourage Russia to demonstrate global leadership. Russia has a lot to offer, particularly in promoting the arms control agenda and supporting nonproliferation. A Russia whose ambitions focus solely on its neighboring regions could be a more difficult partner for the EU.

In 2030 the world will not be a safer place and economic challenges will remain paramount. Russia and the EU—the two most important neighbors—will have few alternatives other than to accept each other as genuine partners, not only to support their own growth and development but also to stabilize the wider region and to address pressing global problems. EU-Russian relations over the twenty years following the collapse of the Soviet Union will be judged as a missed opportunity for partnership, perhaps because both the EU and Russia have been too busy focusing on strengthening themselves—one through enlargement, the other through state consolidation. Nevertheless, the result will be that by 2010, as their geographic proximity has tightened, the two will have become more able to contemplate a real partnership. The 2010–30 period will be crucial for pushing forward a new strategic relationship that capitalizes on the shared interests and goals of both sides and explores pragmatic but limited ways for cooperating within the common neighborhood and beyond.

NOTES

1. In this paper I use the term "the West" to mean the enlarged European Union and the United States. I appreciate, however, that there are significant differences between some EU states and the United States in regard to Russia policy, which will be dealt with later in the chapter.

JONATHAN LAURENCE   **8**

European Islam
in the Year 1451

THE ADVENT OF the twenty-first century was heralded with dark predictions from Ivy League historians, investigative journalists, and Internet populists that, in Europe, the new century would be Islamic.[1] Some argued simply that demography is destiny—that the combination of Muslims' runaway birthrates and European natives' "suicidal" fertility rates would lead to a Western set of Islamic republics by mid-century.[2] Others blamed those hapless Europeans who, by leaving Europe, avoided the good fight: white flight, they argued, had already begun to empty the continent of those who might defend its cultural roots. Moreover, politically correct governments had done little to combat "the dangerous Islamic extremism and culture of death being preached from the mosques of Europe's major cities."[3] In 2009 the futuristic novel *La Mosquée Notre-Dame* predicted that Paris's grandest cathedral would be transformed into a mosque within four decades, and an Italian newspaper crowned Rotterdam the future capital of Eurabia.[4]

Some of that science fiction is based on fact. European women's fertility rates fell in the post–World War II period, and European labor migration and family reunification policies in the late twentieth century led to the exponential growth of a new Muslim minority. But the European

2030 AD corresponds to the Islamic years 1451–52 of the Hegira.

landscape will be etched in less stark relief than the apocalyptic scenarios suggest. In 2030, Islam will continue to be the fastest-growing religion in many parts of Europe—although Evangelical Protestants will likely give Muslims a run for their money in some areas—and many disused churches will have been converted into mosques. As has the sudden growth of the Muslim population, the overnight appearance of minarets will undoubtedly provoke a political backlash. But today there is just one prayer space for every 1,000 to 2,000 or so Muslims, and the rapid increase in prayer spaces will do nothing more than adjust that ratio to match more closely the proportion of Jews and Catholics to existing synagogues and churches. Moreover, in retrospect, it will become clear that many of the manifestations of Muslim radicalism and cultural dislocation are not permanent features of society but the result of a combination of persistent first-generation immigrant issues and the lagging adaptation of European political institutions to second- and third-generation issues.

It does not occur to many critics that Muslims are not always deliberately trying to offend their hosts' sensibilities: that men pray outdoors due to the shortage of mosques; that some slaughter lambs in bathtubs because there are not enough halal abbatoirs; that imams are imported because Islamic theological seminaries have not yet taken root in Europe; that some Muslims took their grievances to the streets because most did not yet have the right to vote. The critics instead seize on the periodic actions of unreformed Islamists to support a catch-22 logic that only delays integration of the Muslim community. The institutional accommodation of Muslims and Islam on an equal basis with other religions, they suggest, would hand a victory to the extremists. Despite their outward endorsement of the diffusion of democracy in the Muslim world, skeptics of Muslims' integration in Europe fail to consider the ways in which internal democratization might strengthen religious moderates in Europe itself.

A number of the social, cultural, and political adjustments that will characterize Europe in 2030 are already under way, although often the results are not visible to the naked eye. The most serious threats—violent extremism among Muslims and right-wing nativism among "host societies"—will ultimately be weakened by the confluence of the old-fashioned social integration process and demographic trends. The key development will be that as the proportion of Muslims of foreign nationality residing in Europe decreases (because the number of native-born

Muslims increases), Europe's democratic political institutions increasingly will kick in. The normalization of Muslims' participation in political life will give a small voice in government to Muslim advocates of all partisan stripes. And the routinization of Islamic religious observance will diminish the significance of religious inequality as a mobilizing issue in Muslim identity politics. National Islam councils will slowly domesticate the religious leadership, rooting it in a European context, and Muslim politicians will gradually be brought into institutional life. Whenever terrorist threats materialize, a plethora of men and women of the European Muslim establishment will stand clearly on the side of democratic societies.

The advent of a large class of voting Muslim citizens will also contribute to the flowering of a rich civil society. The discussions of Muslims' future in Europe and the compatibility of Islam and democracy—that is, of the question "Can Muslims be good citizens?"—will become less abstract, less hypothetical. The answer to that question will no longer be sought in the publicly stated good intentions of Muslim leaders, on one hand, or in the rabble-rousing of nationalists or Islamists prophesying clashes yet to come, on the other. Conflicts over public prayers, unsanitary animal slaughter, and radical proselytizing in prisons and sermonizing in mosques will be addressed and mostly resolved by the practical accommodations and administrative oversight of national interior ministries across the continent. Integration problems will persist, but discussions of how to resolve them will no longer be crudely couched in terms of the clash of civilizations.

In 2030 a small number of European cities will be on the verge of becoming "Muslim majority"—Amsterdam, Bradford, Malmö, Marseille—and one of every four residents in London, Brussels, Paris, and Berlin will have a Muslim background. But as the demographer David Coleman wrote perceptively in 2006:

> The significance would obviously depend on the continued distinctiveness and self-identification of the populations concerned, and on the integration of minorities to native norms, or conversely the mutual adaptation and convergence of all groups. But even on the assumptions presented above, the countries concerned would not become "majority foreign origin"... until the twenty-second century.[5]

As with the advent of "majority-minority" cities in the late-twentieth-century United States, the new demographic configuration in Europe will not have overtly separatist overtones: by 2008, the non-Hispanic white population fell below 60 percent in six U.S. states (including New York) and below 50 percent in four others (including California) without major political disruptions.

Nonetheless, a small number of hardcore anti-integrationist communitarians will persist, and their obstinacy and maximalist demands will likely provide consistent fodder for political leaders with a clash-oriented worldview. The Muslim minority will gamely participate in public and political life, although it will still be underrepresented in national electoral institutions. Yet despite—or because of—the increasing equality of Islam's status as a religion and Muslims' political representation, European countries will witness the rise of nativist challenges. In each country, millions of voters will be receptive to conservative appeals to turn back the clock on Muslim integration into European society. That in turn will lead to low-grade confrontation but not to large-scale social conflict.

DEMOGRAPHY IS DESTINY

Much hay has been made in recent years of provocateurs in the Islamic world who have claimed that "we will conquer Europe . . . not through the sword but through Da'wa [proselytism]"[6] or that "the wombs of Muslim women will ultimately grant us victory in Europe."[7] Yet the year 2030 will come to mark a demographic turning point in a different direction. How will that come to pass, beating the most alarmist forecasts? Just as the growth rates of a developing economy inevitably level off, so too will the Muslim demographic boom. The natural deflation of fertility among women of immigrant origin will take place concurrently with governments' introduction of social policies that create incentives for women to participate in the labor force, which in turn will raise the fertility rates of non-Muslim women in much of western and northern Europe.

The overall EU-25 population will grow slightly until 2025, due to immigration, before starting to drop: from 458 million in 2005 to 469.5 million in 2025 and then to 468.7 million in 2030.[8] The total population

TABLE 8-1. TOTAL POPULATION IN SELECTED EUROPEAN COUNTRIES[a]

Millions

Country	2007	2030
Spain	44.5	45.4
Portugal	10.6	10.7
United Kingdom	60.9	64.4
Ireland	4.3	5.1
France	63.4	65.1
Netherlands	16.4	17.6
Belgium	10.6	11
Luxembourg	0.5	0.6
Germany	82.3	81.1
Sweden	9.1	9.9
Denmark	5.4	5.6
Switzerland	7.5	8.1
Austria	8.3	8.5
Italy	59.1	57.1
Turkey	71	85–90

a. Compiled from Steffen Kröhnert, Iris Hoßmann, and Reiner Klingholz, *Europe's Demographic Future: Growing Regional Imbalances* (Berlin Institute for Population and Development, 2008).

projections showing modest growth in selected European countries (and decreases in Germany and Italy) can be seen in table 8-1.

The population of Muslim background in the EU-25, meanwhile, will increase from 15 million in 2008 to 25 million in 2030, increasing the percentage of Muslims in European countries to more than 6 percent (from 3.7 percent in 2008)—and to as high as 15 to 16 percent in France and Germany (see table 8-2).[9] In 2030 in Britain, all minorities (including non-Muslims) will make up 27 percent of the total population and 36 percent of those less than fourteen years of age.[10]

Women of Muslim background in Europe will still have higher fertility rates than the overall population, but the gap will narrow considerably. In fact, in 2008, signs already appeared that demographic change, while irreversible, would occur less abruptly than feared. The proportion of Muslims will continue to grow, but more slowly as their fertility rates decrease. In 2008, women of North African, West African, or Turkish background in Europe still had higher rates than "native" women—2.3 to 3.3 births per woman—but the fertility rates of foreign-born women were already well below rates of women in their countries of origin. For

TABLE 8-2. LARGEST MUSLIM MINORITIES, NATIONAL ESTIMATES[a]

Percent

Country	2005[b]	2030
France	7.8–8.3	15.2
Germany	3.9–4.3	16.3
United Kingdom[c]	2.9	5.7
Netherlands[d]	5.75	. . .
Spain	2.6	. . .

a. Higher France and Germany estimates are from Richard Jackson and others, *The Graying of the Great Powers: Demography and Geopolitics in the 21st Century* (Washington: Center for Strategic and International Studies, 2008). The authors write that they "assume that the ratio of net immigration to immigrant population will remain constant" and match "fertility rates and age profiles with annual growth rates . . . and then add[] immigration" (pp. 101, 174–75).

b. Lower estimates in 2005 are from "Islam in der Europäischen Union: Was steht für die Zukunft auf dem Spiel? [Islam in the EU: What Is at Stake in the Future?]," Fachreferat Struktur- und Kohäsionspolitik [Structural and Cohesion Policy Unit], Directorate General for Internal Policies of the European Parliament, May 14, 2007.

c. Compiled using figures of 2,700,000 and 3,700,000 Muslims, respectively, from Ceri Peach, "The Muslim Population," in *Muslim Integration*, edited by S. Angenendt and others (Washington: CSIS, 2007), as a percentage of figures from Steffen Kröhnert, Iris Hoßmann, and Reiner Klingholz, *Europe's Demographic Future: Growing Regional Imbalances* (Berlin Institute for Population and Development, 2008), for the U.K. population in 2007 and 2030.

d. David Coleman, "Immigration and Ethnic Change in Low-Fertility Countries: A Third Demographic Transition," *Population and Development Review* 32, no.3 (2006), p.14.

example, the fertility rate of Moroccan-born women in the Netherlands dropped from 4.9 births in 1990 to 2.9 in 2005; that of Turkish-born women fell from 3.2 to 1.9 births in the same period.[11] In Germany in 1990, Muslim women gave birth to two more children, on average, than their native German counterparts; in 1996 the difference was down to 1; and in 2008, it dropped to 0.5. Meanwhile, overall fertility in some western European societies has risen: it rose in the United Kingdom from 1.6 births in 2001 to 1.9 in 2007 and in France from 1.7 in 1993 to the magic replacement number of 2.1 in 2007. There will continue to be lively debate over the influence of family policies on such figures and over whether Muslim women are simply "artificially" propping up Swedish or French fertility rates, both of which increased in 2001–09.[12] Muslim women's total fertility rates are predicted to settle between 1.75 and 2.25 births by 2030.[13]

EU ACCESSION AND DEMOGRAPHY

Because of the European pensioner bulge—the tens of millions of over-sixty-year-olds who were not there a generation earlier—Europe will remain dependent on immigration to help finance what remains of its welfare state and publicly funded retirement plans. Muslim immigration will therefore continue in various guises—high-skilled workers from India, family reunification from Turkey and North Africa, and assorted refugees from those areas—but all new arrivals will be subject to a new regime of stringent and controversial screening that aims to ensure their smooth cultural integration and their economic success. Immigrants will be required to take courses in the official language of their destination country, and they will have to complete a mandatory curriculum on social mores and European history from the Enlightenment through the latest EU treaty.

In 2030, the latest countries to accede to the EU—Croatia, Serbia, Montenegro, and Macedonia (with semi-membership for Iceland and Switzerland)—will increase the EU's base population but will not alter its basic trajectory toward demographic shrinkage. Policymakers will admit that the annual level of net immigration would have to increase two- to threefold to reverse the downward trend in the working-age population.[14] The European Union, therefore, will accomplish several goals by admitting Turkey, with qualified membership, in the late 2020s. (The French president and leaders of several other national governments will have agreed to forego a referendum if the Turks accept a smaller contingent in the European parliament and access to a single rotating commissioner.)

EU enlargement to include Turkey will be used as partial compensation for the continent's gradually shrinking population, allowing it to maintain its share of 6 to 7 percent of the world's population and thus ensuring that it preserves its weight as a "global player."[15] It will also allow chronic labor shortages to continue to be filled by citizens of a country committed to fulfilling the EU *acquis communautaire*. Therefore, even as governments increasingly lean away from Muslim-majority countries for immigration, by 2030 Turkey will provide EU states with their own "internal" source of migration. Moreover, Turkish membership will become a point of pride and a symbol of inclusiveness to the approximately 4 to 5 million residents of Turkish descent living elsewhere in the

EU, massaging a sore spot that has developed during divisive accession talks and threats to hold national referendums on the matter.

Adding Turkey, of course, will also dramatically change the overall Muslim population in the European Union. With a population increase of 25 percent between 2008 and 2030, Turkey will expand to 85 to 90 million, making it the largest single member state—moreover, one with a higher fertility rate and lower age structure than the EU.[16] The share of Muslims in the EU as a whole—including Turkey—will be closer to 20 percent, but net immigration from Turkey to the rest of Europe will not exceed 3 million by 2030.[17]

ELECTORAL POLITICS

How will Europe escape the political alienation of Muslims predicted by so many observers? The central difference between the Muslim populations of 2009 and 2030 will be that most adult Muslims in Europe will be citizens, not third-country nationals. That means that they will no longer simply be the object of policy debates but will increasingly participate in them as full members of society. The vast majority of European Muslims will be enfranchised, they will speak the local language with native proficiency, and their practice of Islam will be set on a course of Europeanization. European political debates about Muslims in 2030 will center mostly on the socioeconomic concerns of an emancipated and enfranchised minority group.

The most striking political development will be the emergence of a small Muslim electorate. Although today's opinion polls show Muslim respondents firmly within the socialist or labor camps in France, Germany, and the United Kingdom, Muslims' political views will evolve to be socially conservative, economically liberal, and dovish on foreign policy. Germany will witness perhaps the most dramatic change. In the 2005 elections, fewer than one in five Muslims enjoyed the right to vote, but the 1999 citizenship law reform—which grants citizenship rights to children born to foreigners as long as one parent is a legal resident—has begun adding 50,000 to 100,000 newborn German citizens of Muslim background a year. The first real generation of native-born German Muslims will begin voting in 2017. Similar trends are under way in France, where 1.5 million to 2 million voters of Muslim background voted in the

2007 national election. By 2030, the number will double to 3 million to 4 million, accounting for just under one of every ten French voters.

In 2030, the major novelty reflecting the electoral and demographic changes of the preceding two decades will be the rise of a handful of openly religious Muslim politicians on nearly every national political scene. The number of single-issue Muslim voters in each constituency will not be able to support a viable "Muslim party," but political parties will begin to open their ranks in earnest to the growing minority after realizing it to be in their own self-interest. Islamic federations in Denmark and the United Kingdom will establish parties that do surprisingly well in local elections. Mainstream parties, already weakened by secularizing trends among nominal Christians and a fissiparous electorate, will be scared into action. Mechanisms for political recruitment from within the electorate of Muslim background will be expanded and nurtured, and spots at the top of candidate lists will be set aside, in practice, for candidates with Muslim surnames. Socially conservative Muslims, who tend to be economically better off and supportive of the political establishment in their grandparents' home countries, will join center-right political parties.

The overtures of mainstream parties will be facilitated also by a pioneering generation of Muslim politicians who speak candidly of reconciling their faith and national citizenship and whose discourses are tailored to the national context in which they operate. In Germany and Italy, they will appeal to the tradition of politician-priests in the period between the First and the Second World War and the advent of Christian Democracy in the wake of the church's expulsion from an official role in public policy. In France and Britain, some Muslim politicians will evoke the precedent set by Jewish statesmen, nineteenth-century figures like French interior minister (and *Alliance Israélite Universelle* president) Adolphe Crémieux or British MP Lionel Rothschild. The victory of President Barack Hussein Obama in U.S. elections will also be cited widely, though it means different things to different people: the limitless possibilities of integration for some, the dulling constraints of Western political systems for others.

Nonetheless, Muslims' transition to full political participation will continue to be a delicate affair. Muslims seeking public office still face an uphill battle. Much of that reflects structural obstacles to newcomers and political outsiders, but in many political contexts, it also indicates a problem with Islam itself, with the best Muslim being an ex-Muslim. The most prominent Muslim in Italian politics—Magdi Allam—has written fierce anti-Islamist tracts and was personally baptized by Pope Benedict; the most prominent Muslim in Dutch politics—Ayaan Hirsi Ali, author of *Infidel*—explicitly rejected her religious upbringing and warned of the threat Islam posed to Western societal norms. Still, the fall of 2008 can be seen as a turning point in the political integration of European Muslims—when Ahmed Aboutaleb was elected mayor of Rotterdam and Cem Özdemir became chairman of the German Green Party. Aboutaleb and Özdemir represent two distinct visions—one religious, one secular—yet both are patriotic and forward thinking. Özdemir is a nonpracticing secularist who married a Catholic woman; Aboutaleb, the son of an imam, is an observant Muslim who proved his bona fides by maintaining excellent relations with the mayor of Amsterdam—his (Jewish) former boss during Aboutaleb's time as deputy mayor there—and by speaking out against separatists and extremists in Muslim communities.

The initiatives to enlarge political coalitions—and voter rolls—will eventually encompass several major factions within Muslim populations. The majority of Muslim voters will align themselves with Socialist and ecological parties, but two other groups will form important minorities. An alliance between remnants of the leftist "antiglobalization" movement and political Islamists will mature, leading to electoral agreements; their foreign policy agenda will seek to reduce the U.S.-European hegemony in the Arab-Muslim world, and they will oppose the terms of Turkish accession and Palestinian statehood. By 2030, the United States and its allies will have long departed from Afghanistan and Iraq, and the Islamists who once railed against blasphemous cartoons and neo-imperialist designs will seem as quaint and harmless as the middle-aged Baader Meinhof and Red Brigades who shuffled from their cells in the early 2000s.

POLITICAL VIEWS OF THE NEW GENERATION

What will Muslim politics look like in twenty years? Will European Muslims be interested in local and national issues or in international affairs and foreign policy affecting Muslims elsewhere? Cross-cutting divisions will certainly expand across the Muslim populations of Europe. The "assimilationists" will argue that European host societies have dropped their most offensive anti-Muslim practices and have begun to open their arms and institutions to Muslims. "Separatists" will contend that Europeans' combination of latent Islamophobia and deep-seated Zionism requires Muslims to withdraw from daily social, political, and economic life and attempt to go it alone by creating enclaves. The separatists will be a small minority, and their ranks will be diminished each electoral cycle by the practical accommodations that national governments offer as incentives for political participation, including experimentation with voluntary shari'a courts to resolve civil disputes.

Nonetheless, the fears that some Muslims have divided loyalties—that they place faith before nation—will not have completely disappeared. Poll results, like those from a 2004 *Guardian* poll, will continue to be cited as proof that a sizable minority of Muslims wants to be governed by shari'a law and supports domestic terrorism. Will Muslims grow inexorably apart from majority societies in 2030? Will they form a "distinct, cohesive and bitter" group?[18]

A 2009 Gallup poll revealed some grounds for optimism in the coming decades.[19] It found that Muslims were more likely to identify with their European homelands than previously thought and that they have slightly more confidence than the overall population in the judiciary and other national institutions. It also showed that 96 to 98 percent of Muslims showed a lack of support for honor killings or crimes of passion, the same percentage as that of the general population. These European Muslims were also revealed to be far more socially conservative by nearly every measure—from the viewing of pornography to the issue of premarital sex.

The 2009 Gallup poll's most thought-provoking section dealt indirectly with the question of tolerance for political violence and terrorism—which is a decent gauge for measuring the differences in political values between Muslims and their "host societies" in future generations. The Gallup poll showed that Muslim attitudes toward civilian deaths were far more nuanced than has sometimes been argued, especially by critics in the United Kingdom. Rather than looking for a yes or no answer, the poll provided a subtler four-point scale measuring degrees of agreement or disagreement and found that between 82 percent and 91 percent of Muslims in Britain, France, and Germany thought that civilian deaths cannot be justified at all.

With regard to the nurturing of a distinct political identity, a dynamic set of membership-based Islamic organizations that cultivate community identification and religious practice will also begin to thrive. Federated at the European, national, regional, and local levels, these organizations will serve as social and political action networks and act as feeders for political and religious associations. Such networks in Europe will owe much, indirectly, to the transnational proselytism of the Muslim World League (MWL) and the twentieth-century exile of various branches of the Muslim Brotherhood (MB), whose envoys and dissidents from Egypt, Syria, Saudi Arabia, and other Gulf states encountered a combination of inviting refugee policies and undefined policies toward Islam in 1960s and 1970s Europe. The dissidents clearing out of Nasserist Egypt, Baathist Syria, and Kemalist Turkey came to pursue advanced degrees and frequently created "Muslim student associations" to campaign for religious rights. But in the year 2030, the generation of Muslim leaders in Europe able to trace their lineage directly to foreign students will have passed the baton to native-born Muslim leaders trained in the youth groups of existing federations.

The transnational and pan-European federations with the most direct links to the MWL and MB will still have only a limited impact on everyday policy discussions and the daily lives of Muslims in Europe. The relevant political space for religious rights, legal recourse for discrimination, electoral influence, and so forth will remain the national stage. European Muslims will still be most affected and influenced by the national federations active in their local and regional areas, since it is those organizations that will be in position to set the policy agenda for authorities to meet.

Many Muslim organizations will be largely irrelevant as actors in state-mosque relations because they are not associated with networks of mosques. Consequently, they will still be excluded for the most part from state-Islam consultations (for example, Conseil Français du Culte Musulman, Deutsche Islamkonferenz, MINAB), which limit official ministerial contacts to mosque administrators and federations of prayer spaces. But the growth of lay Muslim councils to rival religious councils' influence—and often, to overcome the paralysis of the former —will reflect the growing political consciousness of a small but rising Muslim middle class.

Those who participate in activities or occupy leadership positions in Muslim organizations will experience a distinct type of political socialization that will influence their views on national and international debates. They will have been born and raised in Europe and less likely to have lived at great length abroad. They will be less connected to the politics of their ancestral homelands and far less likely to have personal ties to donors in the Gulf and other areas. In the future, therefore, their political affinities will be open to transnational and international influences. Their forums will tend to be critical of U.S. foreign policy, to express continuing solidarity with the Palestinian cause and opposition to Zionism, and to remain vigilant against the rise of Islamophobia in the West. Thus, even when acknowledging the misdeeds of Muslims—in terms of terrorism or anti-Semitism, for example—leaders will tend to be even more worried about the vulnerability to external attack of the Muslim world, from Afghanistan to Iran to Palestine, as well as the still-to-be-consolidated political status of the Muslim minority in Europe. That tendency will fit in with a broader "victimization" narrative (also observable in published materials) and increased publicity of "Islamophobic" incidents when they occur. It will be seen in the context of minority politics, where organizations will have learned from the example of non-Muslim advocacy groups that the best offense is defense. Beyond promoting prayer and Muslim identity, many of the new generation of leadership will be acutely attuned to issues relating to discrimination and prejudice because of their own experiences as university students or young jobseekers or even as just fellow passengers on the metro. Religious leaders will denounce incidences of blasphemy toward Islam, but they will also publicly renounce violence and suggest using the opportunity "to teach someone about Islam" as part of a broader public relations effort or an agenda of proselytism or "re-Islamization."

Overall, organizations in 2030 will demonstrate their independence by freely engaging in political dialogue and compromise more actively than their parents' generation. There will be a considerably greater buzz of interfaith activity with Jewish, Catholic, and Protestant groups. Muslim organizations will be less likely to fall into the kind of erratic behavior that reflects the internal divisions of today; they may nonetheless inherit some of what could be considered the sexist attitudes and the "hate literature"—mostly regarding Jews, Israelis, and Shi'as—of their distant

MWL and MB sponsors. But young people involved in activities at the pan-European level will also be very likely to interact with different-minded people through interfaith weekends and conferences.

Despite community awareness, attempts to build effective foreign policy lobbies on behalf of "Muslim" interests will largely fail. Two major foreign policy developments will have changed the geopolitical landscape: Turkey's accession to the EU and the creation of a Palestinian state. Each event will take place "imperfectly"—that is, critics will suggest that restrictions on the free movement of Turks and Turkey's limited institutional spoils within the European Parliament and Commission mean that Turkey is not really a full member of the EU and that Palestine is only a semi-sovereign state because of regular anti-Islamist raids by military commandoes sent alternately by a NATO rapid-response coalition and the forces of Egyptian president Mubarak (*fils*). But those events will nonetheless be game-changers with regard to the ambitions of Muslim leaders hoping to influence European foreign policy. There will be little consensus among Muslim organizations on common political priorities, especially once the Palestinian question has been partly resolved through the creation of a regional protectorate, helping salve some of the open tensions between France's 10 million Muslims and 1 million Jews. Moderates on the long-standing issue of Kashmir and democratization advocates from Casablanca to Cairo will have been wooed by mainstream parties and convinced of the advantages of the gradualist approach.

SOCIAL INDICATORS

Despite concrete instances of progress in the political realm, social integration will encounter some limitations. In order to reduce the influence of confrontational community leaders who claim Western cards are stacked against Muslims, Europeans will need to address the domestic factors of social and political alienation.

Welfare state reform will hit Muslim-origin families hardest at first but will have a net beneficial impact on Muslims' employment rates overall.[20] Still, fears of a developing Muslim-origin "underclass" will turn out to be well founded—on average, more than 15 percent will be unemployed and collecting meager benefits. That rate will be even higher if national executives do not undertake major prison-building initiatives and pass laws imposing minimum sentences for repeat offenders, drug dealers, and perpetrators of domestic violence. By 2030, Europe's incarcerated population will have ballooned. Although prison populations will still be miniscule compared with those in the United States, Muslim prisoners will make up a majority of the incarcerated and their absolute numbers will have increased considerably.

Disproportionate incarceration and unemployment rates will reflect the continued socioeconomic marginalization of many Muslims in Europe. On that score, the pessimists will be proven right. In 2030 too many young people of Muslim background will fall through the cracks of education reform and affirmative action programs and will, unfortunately, be persistently involved in petty criminality and occasional urban unrest, alongside other economically marginalized subpopulations. They will not be the central thread of the tapestry, but they will be used as an example by skeptics who will continue to argue that Muslims will never fit in or successfully adjust to European society.

Nonetheless, governments will stop the continuous renewal of first-generation problems. That, in turn, will help reduce the "foreignness" of European legal systems and cultural mores. Progress on early education opportunities will steadily improve the basic literacy and linguistic skills of the grandchildren and great-grandchildren of North African and Turkish labor migrants from the mid-twentieth century. Outside of France, English will be increasingly accepted as a second language for Turkish and Arabic speakers. In general, the longtime linguistic "mismatch" between Germans and German immigrants, for example, will begin to resemble the better match enjoyed by people from Belgium, France, Spain, and Portugal and immigrants from the former colonies of those countries, who exhibited greater linguistic homogeneity because immigrants from, for example, former French colonies in Africa were likely to speak French.[21]

Language, however, will increasingly be considered a superficial commonality, insufficient to ensure that the cultural values of migrant groups and host societies overlap. Several countries will continue to restrict the migration of spouses ("import brides"), a constant source of worry for authorities not simply because many such marriages are forcibly arranged but also because the practice repeatedly renews a first-generation situation in which tens of thousands of children are born annually into households without proficient speakers of the host country language. Spouses will have to fulfill age requirements (twenty-three years) and attend a linguistic and cultural training course, with an audio-visual exam at the end (known in migrant circles as the "topless-homo test" because of its explicit images). A black market version of the exam video will be available in many cities of origin, as will advance copies of answer sheets. Women will be advised to avert their eyes at the appropriate points in the video, a tactic not unlike that of the nineteenth-century Jews in Italian ghettos who put wax in their ears when forced to attend church on the Sabbath. Associations representing immigrants will sue governments, arguing that mandatory courses and examinations threaten migrants' cultural heritage, but the European Court of Justice will uphold national government prerogatives in this area.

In the years leading up to 2030, European governments will have made small concessions on the role of religion in the public sphere—for example, by granting limited (and voluntary) jurisdiction of religious law in certain civil cases and laying out fair guidelines on religious clothing in public institutions. In return, governments will require clarity and firmness from community leaders and politicians in public comments supporting national governments' positions on controversial cultural issues such as honor killings and arranged marriages.

In France, after persistent political mobilization by Muslim voters, the headscarf ban will be adapted and reformed during a legislative review process. The law will effectively revert to the spirit of the compromises of the early 1990s, allowing schoolgirls who choose to wear a headscarf to do so during lunch recess. The new law will also unambiguously state the right of all citizens to wear religious garb (with the exception of facial coverings) in public buildings such as city halls. That will have two beneficial effects: one substantive (the outcome will please community leaders) and one having to do with the political process itself (the demonstration that peaceful mobilization can achieve change). But the controversy will also spur the creation of dozens of Islamic schools under association contracts with the state across France, effectively making the issue moot. Muslim parents with the greatest concerns about religious observance will simply send their girls to a subsidized religious school, like their Jewish and Catholic counterparts.

By 2030 the occasional "honor killings" that shocked German and British public opinion during the first decades of Muslim settlement will be classified as hate crimes against women under European law, adding a mandatory additional 50 percent in civil penalties to any criminal sentence. A major EU interfaith program targeting domestic violence across religious communities will also successfully reduce Muslim communities' defensiveness about the cultural problems in their midst.

TERRORISM AND NATIVISM

The most serious challenge to integration will come in the forms of terrorism and nativism. Together, their periodic emergence will threaten to roll back positive social and political developments, especially with more recently settled Muslim populations. A handful of do-it-yourself small-scale terrorist attacks—and one or two large-scale near misses—will take place between 2020 and 2030. For the first time, both the leaders of the terrorist cells and those providing material support will be entirely native born. The shift of European Muslims from "foreigners" to "natives" will carry new risks that require the overhauling of counterterrorism and counterradicalization approaches. The inspiring ideology will still come from abroad, but in 2030, practically every terrorism incident and arrest will be "homegrown." Suspects will be entirely the problem of European governments, which cannot simply deport them to Pakistan or Tunisia, as the U.K. and Italian governments do today. The lasting implication of Islam's Europeanization is that nearly all terrorism suspects will have full rights of citizenship instead of the limited rights of foreign nationals residing on European soil. A greater burden of proof—and controversial legislative reforms—will be required for them to be spied upon, interrogated, or deported. The radicalization threat will not have completely disappeared from the margins of organized religious groups, but the usual policy tools and techniques available for monitoring and countering radicalism among the previously foreign national adult Muslim population will not be available for use on EU citizens.

This development will throw a serious spanner in the works of the much-vaunted counterterrorism practices of Britain, France, and Germany and create new threats to the civil liberties of Muslim-origin citizens. Human rights associations and governments will exchange court cases and victories: a new generation of lawyers will manage to undercut the widespread practice of identity spot checks while governments will gain new detention powers. Caught between the two will be the thousands of new domestic intelligence agents of Muslim origin across Europe. Like the Italian American FBI agents and district attorneys who helped cripple the mafia in U.S. cities, Muslim European agents will help their respective states infiltrate and dismantle violent extremist networks. Police forces and Muslim communities will become increasingly interdependent, and the first Muslim prefects and commissioners will be appointed in a number of European cities. Security agencies in Germany and elsewhere will drop their objections to the formation of Muslim political parties, concentrating instead on providing funding to ensure that they remain well informed on the party leadership's aims and ambitions.

The "naturalization" of Muslims and Islamist terrorism, however, will also increase fears of a fifth column—an "internal enemy" within the EU. The disappearance of Le Pen and Bossi from the political scene in France and Italy, and the failure of their children—Marine and Lorenzo, respectively—to secure subsequent leadership struggles will spell the end of the traditional far right. But nativist movements will have left their mark, especially in Denmark, the Netherlands, Italy, Spain, and the United Kingdom, where elected officials will periodically propose laws requiring referendums on mosque construction and occasionally put forth controversial proposals for mass deportations of illegal migrants from Muslim countries.

RELIGIOUS PRACTICES AND ORGANIZED ISLAM IN 2030

What will European Islam look like in 2030? Will there be a trans-ethnic ummah? The national and regional Islamic councils that all European governments will have put in place by 2010—on a par with the existing practical arrangements for the religious affairs of Jews, Catholics, Protestants, and other faith groups—will help persuade public authorities and public opinion that Islam's expansion is peaceable and that Islam and democracy can coexist. Initiatives such as the Mosques and Imams National Advisory Board in the United Kingdom and the regional branches of the Conseil Français du Culte Musulman in France will mature, and the diffusion of such consultative models to Germany and several other countries will lead to better mutual acquaintance of local prayer leaders and local authorities.

The number of mosques will continue to increase across the continent, so that by 2030 the ratio of Muslims to prayer spaces will be more in line with the ratio of Jews and Catholics to synagogues and churches. Most of the prayer spaces will not be leased facilities but new construction—proper mosques with dome and minaret, built from the ground up.

Europe will still be a generation away from a fully native-born and locally trained imam corps, but for the first time, a slight majority of imams will have received supplemental "civic training" courses offered under the aegis of national integration programs. Hundreds of nationally certified chaplains will serve in European prisons to offer spiritual guidance to Muslim prisoners. Both the funding and personnel for the new prayer spaces will still come largely from abroad, but they will be increasingly channeled through national oversight institutions. Morocco and Turkey will have dramatically increased the number of prayer leaders exported for service in Europe each year, mostly to combat the growing threat of radical imams who collect donations from European congregations to support regime change on the home front. With the expansion of the Iraqi exile population in Europe, Iraq's government will get into the game of Embassy Islam, too.[22] Notwithstanding Mohamed VI's consolidation of power in Morocco, al-Adl wa al-Ihsan's network of social and charitable associations will grow in importance in Europe. And the movement for Kurdish liberation will find religion, transforming the once secular association of Abdullah Öcalan into a serious grassroots religious threat to political stability in southern Turkey and northern Iraq.

The overwhelming majority of fourth- and fifth-generation Muslims in France, Germany, Britain, the Netherlands, and elsewhere will settle into a minority group identity, referring to themselves as "European Muslims" and socializing and engaging in organized political activities with one another across borders. Relations will be tense between the older, established, institutionalized Muslim community and the steady stream of newly arrived first-generation labor migrants from Turkey and North Africa, some of whom will establish their own prayer spaces where they can freely speak their native tongue. The old-country customs of the latter and their inferior knowledge of their host country's language will lead to community rifts, and some native Muslim leaders will look upon them with some condescension and suspicion.

The greatest commonality among national Muslim populations will be their entrenched divisions. National origin will remain a good predictor of piety and politics, although increasing intermarriage between ethnicities (Turkish/Kurdish, Arab/Berber) and nationalities (Turkish/German, Moroccan/Algerian) in addition to intermarriage between Muslims and non-Muslims will confound the simplistic categories of the turn of the twenty-first century. The biggest internal community conflict will be over the role of religion in public life, pitting adherents of political Islam against those who remain loyal to the Embassy Islam of their ancestral countries. The two strains, once predicted to give way to a synthetic "Euro-Islam," will persist in their influence and indeed grow stronger. The internal divisions will harden into lasting cleavages. In most cities, there will be the "Turkish mosque," the "Pakistani mosque," the "Moroccan mosque," and the "political Islamist" mosque, and rarely if ever will the twain meet. In its EU accession talks, the Turkish government will agree informally to incorporate its reformed Turkish Directorate for Religious Affairs (DITIB) into a new directorate for minority religions at the European Commission, which will reach a compromise with Alevite and Kurdish groups to allow their symbolic participation in the drafting of weekly sermons that go out to Europe's thousands of Turkish-sponsored mosques. Such Embassy Islam representatives will generally be the most respectful of host country norms and the separation of state and religion, whereas political Islamists will continue to use institutional means to try to carve out a greater public role for religious expression.

In opinion polls, nearly all European Muslims will say that they fast during Ramadan and that they will make a pilgrimage to Mecca in their lifetime. Mosques on Fridays will not be quite as empty as Catholic and Protestant pews on Sundays, but, like churches, Islamic houses of worship will do their briskest trade on the holiest days of the year. Eid al Adha and Eid al Fitr will be on their way to becoming official holidays in all EU countries that have significant Muslim minorities except Denmark and Italy, although Muslims there may take leave from work. But beyond such superficial religious shared traits, there will be nothing resembling a European ummah.

A European Fatwa Council will come into existence to replace the hodge-podge of Internet imams and pay-as-you-go fatwas. The council will receive endorsements from religious authorities in Egypt, Saudi Arabia, Morocco, and Algeria but will not enjoy full legitimacy. It will aim to achieve the respect of the faithful over time; a Turkish representative will sit in on meetings and may soon apply for full membership. Unlike members of the European Council for Fatwa and Research, a late-twentieth-century creation whose membership was drawn almost entirely from the Muslim world, the majority of the new council's members will be born and bred in Europe, though many of them will have received theological training abroad.

CONCLUSION

Few U.S. policymakers surveying the burning rubble in Chicago, Los Angeles, New York, and Washington, D.C., in the late 1960s could imagine that two African Americans would run the State Department from 2001 to 2009 or that a black family would move into the White House shortly thereafter. The worst tensions in U.S. inner cities were defused by way of an incoherent but effective mix of affirmative action, antidiscrimination policies, interventionist courts, electoral redistricting and reform of party nomination procedures, drug laws, and prison construction. Similarly, by 2030 Europeans will have settled into an acceptance of expanding participation in society and politics, letting democratic institutions do their work and hoping that the economy can support Muslims' entry into the labor market. As long as they make sure that there are good government protections against discrimination and policies promoting participation and educational achievement, they figure that they can hope for the best.

Looking at the skyline of small-town Europe in 2030, it will be hard to recall the virulence with which so many citizen activist groups—patchwork coalitions of secularists made up of prominent ex-Muslims and anticlerical figures—fought mosque construction just decades earlier. Islamist terrorism will have faded as the driving force of policymaking on Muslim issues. As a result, the issue of Muslim integration will be put on a back burner, where it will benefit from being talked about less. Muslim leaders in 2030 will pay tribute to the trailblazers of the earlier generation—

including Wolfgang Schäuble, Giuseppe Pisanu, Jack Straw, Prince Charles, Pierre Joxe, Jean-Pierre Chevènement, and Nicolas Sarkozy—who went out on a limb to assert that Muslims were a permanent component of European societies at a time when it was politically costly to do so. Those statesmen will be memorialized in the cornerstones of large central mosques and the dedication pages of locally printed Qur'ans across the continent.

In 2030, it will have been decades since a great minaret went up over Oxford, fulfilling the eighteenth-century historian Edward Gibbon's prophesy.[23] In fact, every capital city will have its own showcase mosque up and running or in the planning stages. However, those domes and towers will no longer be perceived as the threat to European civilization and its Christian roots that dominated debate at the turn of the twenty-first century. As the twentieth-century French scholar Jacques Berque foretold, just as a distinctive Islam of the Maghreb and an Indonesian Islam developed over time, so too will an Islam of Europe have germinated and begun to grow by 2030.

NOTES

1. Oriana Fallaci, *La rabbia e l'orgoglio* [Rage and Pride] (Milan: Rizzoli, 2006); Bernard Lewis, *Europe and Islam* (Washington: AEI Press, 2007); Niall Ferguson, "The End of Europe?" Bradley Lecture Series, AEI, Washington, March 1, 2004.

2. George Weigel, *The Cube and the Cathedral: Europe, America, and Politics without God* (New York: Basic Books, 2005); see also the YouTube video "Muslim Demographics," which had 7.6 million views as of May 21, 2009 (www.youtube.com/watch?v=6-3X5hIFXYU&feature=related).

3. Quotation from Richard Trank and Marvin Hier, *Ever Again* (Beverly Hills, Calif: Starz/Anchor Bay, 2006); on white flight, see Christopher Caldwell, *Reflections on the Revolution in Europe: Immigration, Islam, and the West* (London: Allen Lane, 2009).

4. Elena Tchoudinova, *La Mosquée Notre-Dame de Paris: année 2048* [The Notre-Dame Mosque of Paris] (Paris: Tatamis, 2009); Giulio Meotti, "Nella casbah di Rotterdam [In the Casbah of Rotterdam]" *Il Foglio*, May 14, 2009, p.1.

5. David Coleman, "Immigration and Ethnic Change in Low-Fertility Countries: A Third Demographic Transition," *Population and Development Review* 32, no.3 (2006), pp. 401–46, p. 422.

6. Phrase attributed to a Muslim Brotherhood spiritual guide, Yusuf Al-Qaradawi. See blog entry, "Islam and American Politics: Deepening the Dialogue" (http://newsweek.washingtonpost.com/onfaith/georgetown/2008/04/west_islam_dialogue.html).

7. Phrase attributed to former Algerian president Houari Boumédiène. See "Houari Boumédiène" (http://fr.myafrica.allafrica.com/view/people/main/id/07QTlFAnWKbU-Coym.html).

8. Green Paper, "Confronting Demographic Change: A New Solidarity between Generations," European Commission, Brussels, March 16, 2005 (http://ec.europa.eu/employment_social/news/2005/mar/comm2005-94_de.pdf). Part of the growth in coming decades will be attributable to net immigration, which in the five largest receiving societies is estimated to total 27.5 million between 2005 and 2050 (national breakdown, in millions: France, 2.7; Germany, 9.1; United Kingdom, 5.9; Italy, 5.4; Spain, 3.0; and Netherlands, 1.4. See Paul Demeny, "Europe's Immigration Challenge in Demographic Perspective," in *Immigration and the Transformation of Europe*, edited by Craig A. Parsons and Timothy M. Smeeding (Cambridge University Press, 2006), p. 38.

9. Projections of the overall Muslim population in Europe for 2005 ranged from 13.8 to 17 million and for 2025 from 25 million to 40 million, although they obviously do not take into account the possibility of Turkish accession to the European Union. In "Global Trends 2025: A Transformed World," released in 2008, the National Intelligence Council sided with the low to medium estimate, saying that if current fertility and immigration rates remain stable, Europe will have a Muslim population of 25–30 million (www.dni.gov/nic/PDF_2025/2025_Global_Trends_Final_Report.pdf). See also "Islam in der Europäischen Union: Was steht für die Zukunft auf dem Spiel? [Islam in the EU: What Is at Stake in the Future?]," Fachreferat Struktur- und Kohäsionspolitik [Structural and Cohesion Policy Unit], Directorate General for Internal Policies of the European Parliament, May 14, 2007.

10. Among those aged sixty-five and older, the minority proportion would be just 11 percent. See Coleman, "Immigration and Ethnic Change in Low-Fertility Countries," p. 422

11. Martin Walker, "The World's New Numbers," *Wilson Quarterly*, May 2009.

12. See Richard Jackson and others, *The Graying of the Great Powers: Demography and Geopolitics in the 21st Century* (Washington: Center for Strategic and International Studies, 2008), and Steffen Kröhnert, Iris Hoßmann, and Reiner Klingholz, *Europe's Demographic Future: Growing Regional Imbalances* (Berlin Institute for Population and Development, 2008), pp. 31 and 131, for different viewpoints.

13. See Ralf E. Ulrich, "Die zukünftige Bevölkerungsstruktur Deutschlands nach Staatsangehörigkeit, Geburtsort und ethnischer Herkunft: Modellrechnung bis 2050 [Germany's Future Population Structure by Nationality, Place of Birth, and Ethnic Origin: A Modeled Outcome until 2050]," erstellt im Auftrag der Unabhängigen Kommission "Zuwanderung" [Commissioned by the Independent Immigration Commission] (Berlin/Windhoek, April 2001); Coleman, "Immigration and Ethnic Change in Low-Fertility Countries; Jackson and others, *The Graying of the Great Powers*.

14. National Intelligence Council, "Global Trends 2025: A Transformed World."

15. Kröhnert, Hoßmann, and Klingholz, *Europe's Demographic Future*, p. 60.

16. "Europe's Changing Population Structure and Its Impact on Relations between the Generations," MEMO/05/96, Brussels, March 17, 2005 (http://europa.eu/rapid/pressReleasesAction.do?reference= MEMO/05/96&format=DOC&aged=1&language=EN&guiLanguage=en).

17. Immigration from Turkey to the rest of the European Union is expected to total between 2.1 and 2.7 million new migrants between 2004 and 2030; Germany will receive roughly half of the new migrants (the higher scenario actually assumes failed accession). See Refik Erzan, Umut Kuzubas, and Nilüfer Yıldız, "Growth and Migration Scenarios: Turkey-EU," EU-Turkey Working Paper 13, Center for European Policy Studies, December 2004 (http://shop.ceps.eu/downfree.php?item_id=1183).

18. Robert Leiken, "Europe's Angry Muslims," *Foreign Affairs* (July–August 2005).

19. See "The Gallup Coexist Index 2009: A Global Study of Interfaith Relations" (www.muslimwestfacts.com/mwf/118249/Gallup-Coexist-Index-2009.aspx).

20. Kröhnert, Hoßmann, and Klingholz, *Europe's Demographic Future,* finds that "as a rule, high levels of social benefits and liberal immigration arrangements . . . are not conducive to an effective integration of immigrants into the labor market" (p. 46).

21. Alicia Adserà and Barry R. Chiswick, "Divergent Patterns in Immigrant Earnings across European Destinations," in *Immigration and the Transformation of Europe,* edited by Craig A. Parsons and Timothy M. Smeeding (Cambridge University Press, 2006), p. 110.

22. "Embassy Islam" refers to mosques and groups controlled by the embassies of the home countries of Muslim immigrant communities in Europe.

23. Ferguson, "The End of Europe?"

Contributors

OKSANA ANTONENKO
Senior Fellow, International Institute for Strategic Studies

JOSÉ MANUEL DURÃO BARROSO
President, European Commission

DANIEL BENJAMIN
Coordinator for Counterterrorism, U.S. Department of State
Former Senior Fellow and Director of the Center on the United States and Europe, Brookings Institution

JOSÉ CUTILEIRO
Former Secretary-General of the Western European Union, Brussels
Former George F. Kennan Professor, Institute for Advanced Study, Princeton University

JOSCHKA FISCHER
Former Minister of Foreign Affairs, Germany

CHARLES GRANT
Director, Center for European Reform

ANDREW HILTON
Director, Centre for the Study of Financial Innovation (CSFI), London

JONATHAN LAURENCE
Senior Fellow, Transatlantic Academy, German Marshall Fund
Assistant Professor of Political Science, Boston College
Nonresident Senior Fellow, Brookings Institution

RUI CHANCERELLE DE MACHETE
Constitutional and Administrative Attorney
Former Minister of Justice of the IX Constitutional Government
Former Deputy Prime Minister and Minister of Defense of the IX Constitutional Government

HUBERT VÉDRINE
Former Minister of Foreign Affairs, France

JOSEPH H. H. WEILER
Professor, European Union Jean Monnet Chair, New York University

Index